The Value Industry

Daniel Barnes

The Value Industry:
Reflections on Art, Money and Celebrity

Daniel Barnes

N e w T h e y
London and Margate
2019

ISBN: 1724355759
ISBN-13: 978-1724355751

N e w T h e y Publishing, London and Margate, with CreateSpace and
Kindle Direct Publishing by Amazon

Cover image by Jon Christopher
Design by N e w T h e y

For Rosie Mai, Willow, Ella and India

and Zizi

Contents

Preface

This book is about the relationship between art and money. The central question concerns how we deal with the entanglement of culture with capitalism, of art and economics, and how art can survive it. The book came into being through the fortuitous convergence of a trinity of unconnected events on the evening of 15 September 2008. That amazing cosmic coincidence, for all its romance and caprice, brought about this very project.

On that fateful evening, in Nottingham, tattered and frayed from years of isolated toil, I was preparing the final version of my PhD thesis to send to the printers the next day. In London, Damien Hirst was playing snooker with Ronnie O'Sullivan, while across town Sotheby's was selling 223 lots of artworks that had never been shown in a gallery. And in New York City, Lehman Brothers was dealing with the fallout from filing for Chapter 11 bankruptcy. The Great Crash of 2008 had begun, and myself and Damien Hirst would forever be entwined in its wake.

I realised I had to write about the relationship between art and money precisely because art seemed so curiously resistant to recession. In 1997, Britain was awash with an unusual optimism. The Labour party promised that things could only get better and things did get better – we all got a little bit wealthier because we were offered oodles of delicious credit. We were a more educated, more affluent, modern nation of home-owners and art-lovers than ever before. So, it was no wonder that the assembled crowd at Sotheby's on the night of the Great Crash thought nothing of splurging a couple of million on a dead thing that wanted nothing more than to be left alone to rot. Damien Hirst had the last laugh, not just at those collectors, but at the whole creaking mechanism of the world economy.

The crisis cut deep and wide, ravaging everything that capitalism holds dear, and yet, like God guiding the hand of Abraham, it hardly seemed to so much as scuff the art market. There were fallow years in 2008 and 2009, and then again in 2015 and 2016, but a lot of money was still spent on art, especially considering there was a recession on. In any case, aside from the predictable plummet immediately following the Great Crash, art made quite a show of a speedy recovery. It made a mockery of the slow progress elsewhere. Art, it seemed, suffered a great deal less than the rest of us. It was as if the collectors were cockroaches: immune to the radiation of nuclear fallout, they still found the money to pay Hirst, and then some.

In fact, the Great Crash had a seemingly contradictory, but entirely logical, effect on the art market. It made some people behave as if nothing had happened, and it inclined some people to work harder. At one end of the scale, the One Percent retained their billions and continued to buy art, so that galleries and auction houses continued a brisk trade while everyone else was flailing in the gutter.

At the other end of the scale, it was a different story, for while the very richest continued to buy the very most expensive art, recession hit smaller and mid-sized galleries who depended, not on the disgustingly wealthy, but on the tastefully affluent. They were the kinds of galleries which needed a constant trade to keep afloat because they too were battling the ever-increasing cost of existing. They were the kinds of galleries whose clients were not so super rich that they kept spending when the chips were down.

You would think that, when times are lean, art would be the first thing to go as so much luxury. But throughout the recession, the richest continued to buy art. I am not saying that the artworld did not suffer in the recession, but I am saying that the total amount spent on art in 2009 – which was its lowest point throughout the whole recession – was still around €29,000,000,000. That is less than previous years, but, remarkably, it is still more than at any point in history prior to 2006. The reason for this is that while the richest continued to make, sell and buy art, the poorer artists, critics and curators, throughout the worst of times – perhaps even *because of* the worst of times – simply kept working regardless of whether they were being paid because they were driven by passion. Consequently, the artworld subsisted on the intoxicating mixture of billionaires' bank accounts and the paupers' pure love of art.

The combined effect of the poor working hard for their very survival and the rich spending hard as if nothing had happened was that market confidence remained unharmed. Like any market, art stands or falls on confidence, and that is precisely what happened throughout the recession – everybody carried on as if everything was fine, so the market took this as a sign that everything really was fine. If the billionaires had stopped buying or the struggling artists had stopping putting on exhibitions, then maybe the market would have trembled, but nobody did any such thing, so art powered on ahead while homes were being repossessed and jobs were vanishing into thin air.

This book is a product of that struggle. When I finished my PhD, even universities were cutting back and the chances of an academic job diminished by the hour. Eventually, I gave up and decided to become a penniless art critic. This eventually led me to a menial role within a world-class commercial gallery, where I whiled away many happy years doing nothing of consequence but having a great time being part of the theatre of the commercial artworld at its highest level. It was during that time, at the tiny Gagosian in Davies Street, London, that I saw Damien Hirst's 'Poisons and Remedies' (2010) with my inspirational friend, Leon. The exhibition fascinated me as the epitome of art's resistance to recession – here was some mildly interesting and aesthetically riveting, but not thereby earth-shattering, art which was set to sell for more money than I was likely to make over the course of the next two decades. Leon and I shared that sense of awe with equal measure of abandon and cynicism, which is way he was and remains a great friend and a great muse. And then I remembered how, as I was chipping away at my PhD thesis, that sale at Sotheby's had gripped me so tightly even though, at that time, I had no notion of what it meant in the grand scheme of either art or my own life. This, I thought, required a philosopher to unpack the mystery of why art and money have such a fruitful relationship.

It will not go unnoticed that I predominantly focus on glitzy blue-chip art made by superstar artists and sold by mega-rich dealers to super-rich collectors. The reason for this narrow focus, and for ignoring all the extremely good non-commercial art out there, is that it is in the commercial artworld that questions of value are posed so loudly and yet silenced so efficiently. In subjecting art to serious critical reflection, a philosopher is, to paraphrase Hegel, acting like a deaf person who is answering a question the artworld has not asked.

In response to that silence, from January 2014 to December 2015, I wrote a column called 'Value and Ideas' for *FAD Magazine*. In those articles, I offered philosophical responses to news stories about the humdrum madness of the commercial artworld in an attempt to explain how art and money work together. Those articles formed the bulk of the research for this book, in addition to working for a gallery, where I witnessed first-hand the daily ballet of buying and selling.

So, here we are at the sharp end of a series of coincidences, which resulted in this book. Lehman Brothers caused the recession, which caused me to turn from academic philosophy to art; Hirst helped art to flourish in recession, which inspired me to write my column and, ultimately, this book. Consider the counterfactuals: if that shocking display had never occurred at Sotheby's, perhaps I would never have been seduced by Hirst; or if Lehman Brothers had not handed out subprime mortgages as if they were ice lollies, perhaps art would have taken a new direction altogether for purely cultural reasons; or if art had crashed too, perhaps none us would be here doing any of this. But all those things did happen, and we all survived. It is as if, in the words of Kurt Vonnegut Jnr, 'everything was beautiful and nothing hurt'.

Daniel Barnes

DJB, July 2019

I. An Impossible Proposition

Two kinds of value, one kind of problem

It is more difficult than ever to tell the difference between important art and expensive art, real art and a mere simulation, clever art and banality. But it is possible. If we grasp with both hands the elusive concept of value, if we can untangle the relationship between art and money, we can see clearly the difference between art which is good because it expensive and art which is expensive because it is good. The tussle between quality and price is just one way in which the value industry – the vehicle by which value is created from almost nothing of worth – makes us think that art is both nothing more than a mere commodity and anything but that.

At one point in time, in the foyer of Christie's HQ in New York, standing at over nineteen feet tall and made of painted steel, Jeff Koons' *Balloon Monkey (Orange)* (2006-2013) presided over daily business. Something that, at first sight, appeared to be another monumental Koons sculpture, turned out to be so much more. According to artist and curator, Robert Storr, it was a grisly metaphor for the art market – an inflatable thing that cannot be deflated[1]. As we shall see, it is that and so much more.

The Value Industry

Contemporary art is an extremely multifaceted thing, for whilst it is more than pickled sharks and unmade beds, it is also more than a romantic myth or a simple pleasure. Art is an integral part of mass culture and a commodity on a market which claims to be the arbiter of value. But although there often seems to be a mismatch between the price of art and its cultural worth, the humdrum madness of the artworld still preserves what is centrally valuable and worthwhile about art, namely that it is a source of intellectual stimulation and aesthetic pleasure.

Nonetheless, contemporary art is in crisis: so much of what appears in galleries is fodder for the market, designed to fill space and time with confections and conceits to line the pockets of dealers and artists. This is due, in no small measure, to the operation of the value industry, which creates value only to sell it on for profit, circular and maddening forever. Value is concocted from thin air; it is just numbers in the ether, the ghost in the machine; it is reason and passion, but remains fluid, slippery and insidiously efficacious. The art which commands such high prices is, after all, more often than not made from cheap materials of at best pedestrian interest and value. And yet, when touched by the hands of an artist, this workaday matter – some household gloss paint, a dead fly, an old patchwork blanket – becomes art, and becomes valuable.

[1] Quoted in Charlotte Burns, 'Year of Record Sales, But at What Cost to the Art?', *The Art Newspaper*, issue 246, January 2015.

Arthur Danto, the singular apprehender of the philosophical nature of art, stated it perfectly when ruminating on Warhol's Brillo boxes: 'Is this man a kind of Midas, turning whatever he touches into the gold of pure art? And the whole world consisting of latent artworks waiting, like the bread and wine of reality, to be transfigured, through some dark mystery, into the indiscernible flesh and blood of the sacrament?'[2]. Art, he thought, is not magic or miracle, but it certainly seems that way when something that looks like a mere Brillo box suddenly becomes valuable. At the time when Danto was writing and Warhol was just becoming famous, in 1964, the world was looking at the tip of a very large iceberg that only grew ever more unavoidable as the seas of art were frozen by ever more money and fervour.

Intensive, prolonged exposure to contemporary art and the market leads one to realise that art is all about value precisely because nobody knows what value is. With this essential gap in our knowledge, the market can trade in the conceit that value is simultaneously intrinsic to art and extrinsic to anyone's understanding of it, so the product always comes with in-built philosophical mystery.

In order to get to grips with how and why art is valuable, even when it is irreducibly locked into the framework of money and celebrity, it is necessary to see value as operating at two levels, as derived from the work of Isabelle Graw[3]. First, there is cultural value, which is a measure of the significance of something's contribution to human culture and is therefore valued in and of itself as art; and second, there is economic value, which is the price an artwork must have for the purpose

---

[2] Arthur C Danto, 'The Artworld' *Journal of Philosophy* LXI, p. 571-584, (1964), 580-581.

[3] Isabelle Graw, *High Price: Art between the Market and Celebrity Culture* (Berlin: Sternberg Press, 2009).

of exchange, since art must be exchanged. This distinction is derived from Graw with some modification, who uses the terminology 'symbolic' and 'market' value. However, 'symbolic' sounds too mystical, as if we are buying into a notion of art as some kind of magic, as certain overly-romanticised notions of art might hold. Moreover, to speak of symbolism is to privilege the semantic content of art, and while meaning is important, the contention here is that art is centrally and primarily an aesthetic phenomenon. 'Market', on the other hand, is too narrow a term, restricting value to something like exchange-value, which bypasses the importance of the pure, abstract concept of value in the economics of art. Thus, we will use the terms 'cultural' and 'economic' value, but still ultimately preserving the essential flavour of Graw's distinction. Given that these two kinds of value are real and present in contemporary art, it is necessary to investigate the links between them, as well as to explore the points at which they diverge.

Cultural value, in particular, is a slippery customer, but it is worth starting with the notion that the value to culture of a work of art is not entirely subjective. Individuals may have their perceptions of a given work's cultural value, but the true sense of cultural value is significantly more Kantian in nature. Cultural value will be more or less organically agreed upon, since a work of art will exude such qualities that independent observers will agree about the work's significance and they will thus predict its endurance. A single person's judgement of cultural value may not be incorrect, but it is not enough. However, economic value requires the agreement of at least two people – buyer and seller – in order to possess the requisite legitimacy for its operation. The fundamental cultural significance of a work or an artist is something that – if it truly exists – disparate people will perceive and agree on, even if they agree on nothing else about the work or artist. Cultural value is as elusive as it sounds, but we can take solace in the fact that it unfolds organically and effortlessly in the course of everyday aesthetic judgements.

The fact is that the contemporary artworld does not make sense as either an economic or cultural proposition: there is too much money for it to be about art, but there is too much art for it to be about money. Once we see contemporary art through the lens of a pervasive tension between cultural and economic value, we begin to make sense of things that are otherwise baffling: how Damien Hirst can command the destruction of a Spot Paining, why it is important to save Tracey Emin's bed, how a fake Richter can be as valuable as a genuine one, and why celebrities who make bad art are erroneously considered worthy artists.

The artworld's impossible proposition is this: the artworld is a multi-billion-dollar industry, safer than oil and equities, and yet it is the machine that produces the next Picasso and adorns our museums with the wonders of the future's past. It is only by untangling the concept of value that we can begin to resolve this impossible proposition into something palatable which accurately characterises how we engage with contemporary art.

The fact of culture's entanglement with economics is obscured by an operative mythology, wholly propagated by the art establishment. That is, the strife between culture and economics – and therefore the foibles, inconsistencies and injustices of their union – is glossed over on an industrial scale by gallerists, curators, auction houses, critics and artists who weave the myth that there is no essential tension between culture and economics. When you go to an exhibition at a commercial gallery, it is presented as just that – an exhibition –

and not a sales pitch or an investment opportunity. The myth of the harmonious union of art and money blurs the lines between cultural and economic value so assiduously that we hardly notice the tectonic plates shifting in favour of money, so when the history is written it will all have been worth every penny.

The reason for this is that we must believe in the market's power to maintain a positive role in the artworld: although the market is, as markets always are, all about money, that money is sustaining the existence of art, which is a sovereign good. Thus, so the myth says, the art market is eternally justified by its continued contribution to culture. Moreover, a sufficiently complex and/or well-marketed myth can compensate for, even gloss over, the fact that beyond the myth there is almost nothing of value. Nonetheless, the prevailing mythology, like the prevailing wind, carries the ship of commercial success along as if on its own steam.

Aesthetics is simultaneously part of this mythology and an antagonist to it. It is only the singularity of aesthetics in human interests that justifies the existence of art. The myth of the goodness of the market aims to preserve this, but that endeavour is fraught with tension. Aesthetics is important because it is a central way in which we apprehend the world; it is through aesthetics that we seek and discover meaning, expression and, ultimately, pleasure. This conception of aesthetics is brilliantly summed up by Matthew Collings, who says 'art is partly ideas and theories, but it is only anything at all because of the way it looks'[4]. That is, the way art looks is the locus of what it means, what it makes us feel, what it makes us think, how it affects our lives, the pleasure or pain it elicits and the very reason we bother with art at all. The problem comes

---

[4] Matthew Collings, *The Rules of Abstraction* (BBC Four: 4 September 2014).

when we consider that, on the one hand, aesthetics transcends economic principles, and, on the other hand, it must be co-opted by them if art is to be a commodity. As such, the mythology of 'the Artist' or something like 'aesthetic experience' as romantic cornerstones of humanity are weaved, sometimes incongruously, into the fabric of the art market. As Graw says, the economics of art is predicated upon the idea of putting a price on the priceless. The great coup is that very often it works. And we can only unveil this coup if we apply the distinction between cultural and economic value to the great mystery of contemporary art: how the artworld creates value out of almost nothing at all and how the practice of contemporary art became the value industry.

Since aesthetics is the First Principle of art, the gateway to meaning and value, ruminations on value often take it as a given, as something always already apprehended when we make any judgement at all, even if we are sometimes given to think that aesthetics is a mystery that can only be unlocked through esoteric means. From this theoretical standpoint, commercial art generally looks a great deal better, and as Bret Easton Ellis said, 'the better you look, the more you see'[5].

Art is valuable because it is aesthetically desirable and it is worth remembering that it is this, and this alone, that the market is putting a price on. All the money, celebrity and spectacle that we see unfurled daily in the name of art is in some ways essential to it, since contemporary art can only be the product of its socio-historical epoch, but it is also a smokescreen which capitalism has developed in order to justify

---

[5] This is the catchphrase of the protagonist in *Glamorama*, a privileged kid who nominally works as a model and a club-owner. The character's conceit is twofold: first, looking carefully yields better results, and second, privilege entails that you are entitled to see more than others. A perfect analogy for the artworld. See Bret Easton Ellis, *Glamorama* (London: Picador, 1998).

the madness of the market. Underneath all of that there are aesthetic ideas which are operating even where they seem so impossible – in the mind of Jeff Koons, in the pockets of Charles Saatchi and in the halls of Gagosian.

Theodore Adorno said that the culture industry is abominable mass deception, which occurs when culture gives in to the allure of mass production[6]. The primary illustration of this phenomenon, which, in the early 20th Century, swept through every facet of culture, was the advent of audio-visual recording. According to Walter Benjamin, it hailed the mechanical reproducibility of art, which spawned a whole new industry in which culture could be produced and exchanged on a mass scale[7]. For Adorno and Horkheimer, this spelled trouble for so-called high art – music, painting, poetry – because it gave the masses easy access to so-called low culture, such as cinema and popular music, that they would fail to engage with high art altogether. The situation today is even worse than an irascible grump like Adorno could have imagined, for what we used to high-mindedly call the 'culture industry' has morphed under the dual powers of postmodernism and capitalism into something altogether more sinister. We now have a value industry, which displays a blithe indifference to culture and yet still manages to produce something that remarkably resembles it.

The value industry is a step beyond its forbear, the culture industry, in one crucial respect: it is the product of postmodernism, which flattened the contours of culture, blurred the lines between high and low art until this culture

---

[6] See Theodore W Adorno and Max Horkheimer, 'The Culture Industry', in *Dialectic of Enlightenment*, trans. John Cumming (London: Verso, 1997).

[7] Walter Benjamin, 'The Work of Art in the Age of Mechanical Reproduction', in *Illuminations,* trans. Harry Zorn (London: Pimlico, 1999).

industry is all we have[8]. In the culture industry, everything, from cinema to music, claimed to be culture, but it was not, according to Adorno and Horkheimer, of equal value. Rather, they said, within this mass of generic culture, there was a distinction between high and low culture, with the former being gold and the latter mere slurry. This was before postmodernism. One of the central characteristics of postmodernism is the structural flattening of the contours of culture, so that 'low' culture became high. For example, on the swish of Warhol's magic whip, the gutter art of advertising illustration – practiced only by failed artists and charlatans – was elevated to the echelons of high art (fine art, as we call it) with the Brillo box and Campbell's soup can. The culture industry had been usurped by a value industry that now gave low culture high status and, ultimately, high value.

The value industry thus emerges at precisely the point when Warhol begins to put a high value on low culture[9]. The main product is now not culture at all, but pure, abstract, value. It is about producing something that will be valuable to both the masses (i.e. cultural value to the audience) and to the elite (i.e. economic value to the collectors and the art market). It is, as Danto said, turning everyday materials into the gold of art. Then, suddenly, everything is (potentially, at least) valuable and there is no distinction between high and low culture because, as Pop Art, neo-expressionism and the YBAs would go on to demonstrate again and again, anything can be

---

[8] For such an account of culture, see Fredric Jameson, 'Postmodernism and Consumer Society', in *The Cultural Turn* (London: Verso, 2009).

[9] The practice of taking the everyday and elevating it to the status of art begins, of course, with Duchamp, but Warhol was the first to actively and successfully monetise it. See Chapter 4 for more on this.

transfigured into culture, and therefore into pure value. That is the value industry in which we now operate[10].

It is thus no longer the artefacts of culture – films, music, paintings, poems – that are of interest, for the culture industry produced them for their own sake, but it is the pure, abstract concept of value that is of primary interest. The value industry produces artefacts of culture almost incidentally as the bearers of this pure, abstract value, not unlike the bread and wine that are the sacramental bearers of the blood and body of Christ. In the art market, nobody cares much about the aesthetic difference between one Richter and another, or the distinct aesthetic import of a Doig and a Pollock, but only about the differences in value that can be discerned between them.

These differences in value may very often have nothing whatsoever to do with anything the artist did or intended, but will nonetheless be irreducibly attached to the work by the operations of the market which, in the final analysis, is more interested in the dissemination of value than in the redistribution of aesthetic edification. Even in the in the wake of Warhol's emergence, but significantly before the industrial commodification of contemporary art, John Berger smelt a rat in the artworld's claim to uniqueness. Echoing Benjamin, he said, 'The bogus religiosity which now surrounds original works of art, and which is ultimately dependent on their market value, has become the substitute for what paintings lost when the camera made them reproducible'[11]. Berger is worried about the aura of the painting, as Benjamin would put it, being dissolved in the fog of reproduction by photography, but his

---

[10] For example, the very fact that a blog – a collection of mindless opinions written online by a nobody for no reason other than self-indulgence – can make money typifies the 21st Century stage of the value industry.

[11] John Berger, *Ways of Seeing* (London: Penguin, 1972), 23.

point reaches still further than he, at the time, might have imagined. The value industry holds reproducibility above everything else, for value is conceived in terms of the number of units available to sell. A Richter abstract is valuable precisely because it is *one of the Richter abstracts* – in owing it, the collector is a member of an exclusive club. According to the value industry, it is better to be a member of the club than a lone wolf because you possess a commodity which can be sold, if the mood takes you; so you are therefore always already a potential business partner for dealers and auction houses. If, conversely, you possess a unique Rembrandt self-portrait you may well gain kudos from being the only member of your club, but you are not a potential vendor – since you are supposed to have no desire to sell – and therefore the value industry has no use for you. Reproducibility is the core business of the value industry because it – unlike uniqueness or originality – guarantees the indefinite continuation of business. Consequently, the esteem in which some may hold a Richter abstract is and can only ever be, as Berger says, bogus religiosity, since there are hundreds more where that came from, and, probably, hundreds more to come.

We can believe in contemporary art only if we understand it as a product of this capitalist machine that seeks to produce, above all else, value. It is a machine which fashions value out of dust, detritus and dreams, or anything that can be monetised and marketed under the guise of culture. The value industry says, 'If you can dream it, it can be made. If you can make it, it can be sold!'. And so, Tracey Emin unmakes her bed and Martin Creed forgets to fix a faulty light-fitting and value is conjured from almost literally nothing.

Ever optimistic, we will see that art survives the market precisely because it is absolutely necessary to humanity, whereas the market is only ever contingent. That is, in a society where we do not have formal mechanisms of unequal exchange such as markets, we would still sing songs, draw pictures and tell stories[12]. This is because art is an essential part of the fabric of what it is to be human, no matter what price can be put upon it and no matter how much rich critical prose can be written about it.

For the Love of Art and Money

The massive amount of money that circulates within the artworld, and the inequality it breeds, is in strife with the core purpose of art. This, however, is not new; it is entrenched in the history of art itself and does nothing to change what we centrally value in art, even if it sometimes moulds it.

The relationship between art and money is assiduous: money is both necessary to the very existence of art in capitalist societies; and it is a mortal threat to art's integrity. This cannot simply be attributed to the onward march of global capitalism or to the lust of art dealers; rather, something happened in art itself that was the catalyst for it all. Let us take a moment to tell this crushing love story and to think about how we, the contemporary artworld's impoverished children, might best deal with the tricky relationship that has spawned us.

A collection of 8601 diamonds[13] signalled the moment that the romance between art and money had finally gone too

---

[12] This notion is elucidated by Matt Ridley, *The Rational Optimist* (London: Fourth Estate, 2011).
[13] This is the number of diamonds that comprise Damien Hirst's *For the Love of God* (2007).

far[14.] We knew there was something seriously askew when, one evening in 2007 on BBC2's *Newsnight*, an appalled Kirsty Wark pointedly challenged an obstinate, baffled Damien Hirst with the question: '£14,000,000 worth of diamonds and platinum. Is there nothing in your mind that thinks there's something obscene about that?' That was the moment when an entire generation, like those who witnessed the art booms of the 80s and 60s, saw art and money for what they really are. It was obscene, and yet nobody was prepared to admit it; instead, it was celebrated as the pinnacle of artistic achievement.

But it was Warhol who cast the spell. First, he invented the value industry, as we have seen, by making high art about low culture. This new art enchanted the artworld with its sheer ordinariness, giving artworks the status, in the consumer society, of both luxury goods and mystifying reflections of society itself. And second, he contrived his studio to emulate industrial mass-production by delegating the work to assistants, speeding up the rate of production. This was art's industrial revolution, which led to the 1980s when the prices of high-rollers like Basquiat, Kiefer, Schnabel and Koons began to rocket. Then, in the 90s, it happened all over again with the YBAs.

This is how the star-crossed lovers met: Warhol introduced Art to Money on a blind date over a Brillo box; they embarked on a whirlwind romance before getting married, battled in sickness and in health to spawn many wayward children along the way. And to this day, they are still very much in love.

In 1990, the global art market was worth $27,000,000,000, and in 2007, before the Great Crash, it was closer to

---

[14] See Chapter 5, The Pay Me Girl Has Had Enough of the Bleeps, for more on this.

€48,100,000,000. Interestingly, after the Crash the art market remained largely unharmed, dipping somewhat in 2008 and 2009, only to swiftly recover with global sales totalling €43,000,000,000 in 2010. In 2011, that figure crept up again, signalling another year of steady growth, with art outperforming equities markets, reaching €46,100,000,000. On 12 November 2014, Christies New York set the world record for total sales in a single auction at $852,887,000, in its Post War and Contemporary evening sale[15]. The total for 2014, following years of growth, was €51,000,000,000, which preceded a couple of years of decline, only for the market to recover to its highest value yet this century, coming in at €56,600,000,000 in 2017[16]. These numbers are beguiling. Even if you silence the fact that art proved perversely immune to global recession, there is the unfathomable fact that only a small handful people, out of everybody in the world, spent that €56,600,000,000.

The blunt end of these numbers is the fact that art is just stuff: not stuff like minerals or oil which are expensive to produce, since most art is made from cheap, readily available materials; it is not stuff like food or construction materials where that amount of money sustains so much life; and it is not even luxury stuff like Armani suits that cost more than a Ferrari but can be put to good use daily. Art must have its kudos constructed in critical acts of convolution, and it is stuff which – for the most part – is only experienced fleetingly and

---

[15] Prior to that, the record was set by the November evening sale a year earlier, when in 2013 Christies New York totalled $691,000,000, including $142,000,000 for Francis Bacon's *Three Studies of Lucian Freud* (1969).

[16] All these figures are taken from the TEFAF Report which, until its demise in 2018, was considered the authority on quantifying the value of the global art market. The report was produced by The European Fine Art Fair in Maastricht, the Netherlands.

by relatively few. It is not that art is inconsequential, but just that, given the grand scheme of stuff, its global market value is a baffling affectation of modern life, given the position of art in the grand scheme of things.

These global sales figures, which cause apoplexy and hubris in equal measure, are the work of auction houses, private sales and commercial galleries. These sales involve not only a miniscule fraction of all the people living in the world, but also a tiny portion of those people who make up the global artworld. After all, it is the richest – the One Percent – who are buying most of the art. And it is towards these people that much of the value industry's energy is directed, since economic value is concocted and inflated precisely so that collectors will pay astronomical prices. The value is created, therefore, so that the value can be realised. The artworld, as far as money is concerned, is a petulant microcosm of all the world's inequality and injustice.

Graw characterises the art market as a form of 'cognitive capitalism', whereby knowledge has inherent, marketable value, so the price of an artefact is justified by the intellectual acumen attached to it[17]. So artworks have a dual nature, she says, following Bourdieu, as a cultural asset and a commodity: the two are separate and interlinked in such a way that cultural value makes the artwork priceless, but economic value ensures that it must necessarily have a price. The problem, then, is that prices dominate culture – we always hear from auctions and gallery openings about what sold and for how much, never anything about the meaning, aesthetics or history of the works.

Furthermore, the artworld includes a large majority who do not make money from art; who, in fact, barely make a living. The graduate artists, the budding critics and wannabe

---

[17] See Graw, *High Price*, Chapter 1.

curators often work for free; sometimes they are lucky enough to complete menial tasks on a zero hours contract or to command a miniscule fee for their talents from someone who resents paying them at all. But overall, in art as in life, the only people making money are the ones who already have it, with no extant mechanism for redressing the imbalance.

Given that the artworld is a shining beacon of inequality and that we do not want to give it up altogether in some eternally pious cultural Lent, we need a new way of thinking. A new way which does not obsess over the numbers and inequality. The money surely makes a lot of art possible, and that is for the good of all of us, since art is there for all and it is eternally ours for the taking, no matter which billionaire claims they own it. It is this cultural value which should always trump that economic value, not least because ownership is an illusion since art outlives both a collector and their money.

The love story of art and money is set to run and run like a great soap opera, and although it seems toxic, it is subsidiary to the main plotline about our own magical affair with art, which relieves the tedium of our crushing lives under late capitalism. But let us pause to consider the genesis of this story and to see how the relationship between art and money flourished in London the dying days the 20th Century.

The Genesis of a Fable

Suppose, for a moment, there was a time when art was expensive because it was good. This mythical kind of art fitted in to a traditional model of fine art as painting and sculpture that had mimesis as its aim. Suppose, then, that in this world the price of a work of art reflected the ingenuity that went into crafting landscapes, portraits, religious icons, images of royalty, peasants and pastoral scenes. This is the world, in terms of painting, of Caravaggio, Rembrandt and Leonardo, through to van Gogh, Constable and Turner, and ending with Freud, Bacon and Auerbach. In this world, the price of art was an extraordinarily reasonable creature, since the price you paid reflected a genius most could hardly dream of possessing.

The difference between that world and the world of the value industry is that in the latter art is expensive, not because it is good, but because it is irreducibly entrenched in a world of capitalism and celebrity. Granted, the nature of art has changed, so a new art necessitated a new pricing structure, but perfect resemblance or exquisite representations were no longer the order of the day, so art began to be priced according to its conceptual content or aesthetic impact. And this, since it could not be located in craft or skill, seemed a great deal less reasonable. Although the world of reasonable prices and artistic genius is a theoretical conceit, to imagine it is to grasp the idea that the value industry, as it is construed here, has not always existed, and that, before its inception the value of art was a very different creature from that which it is now.

The birth of the global value industry, as we have seen, occurred in the 1960s when Warhol began to manufacture art, but in the UK, it matured very late. In the late 1980s, the London artworld consisted of just a few galleries, which mainly showed American or German art, situated around Mayfair's Cork Street. This arrangement possessed no mechanism by which young artists could flourish and the general public could engage with contemporary art. A revolution was needed to reinvigorate an artworld that had been stagnating since the golden days of Freud and Bacon, and to revitalise a country languishing on the edge of depression[18]. British art was yet to spawn homegrown talent with the power to dominate the market and thus to create a distinct strand of the value industry which could claim London as the epicentre.

In the late 80s and early 90s, a distinct group of artists emerged from Britain's art schools. Goldsmiths College of Art, South East London, was the epicentre of the revolution: it produced Damien Hirst, Marcus Harvey, Sam Taylor-Johnson, Michael Landy, Fiona Rae, Mat Collishaw, Gary Hume, Angus Fairhurst, Gillian Wearing and Sarah Lucas. The Royal College of Art produced Tracey Emin, Jake and Dinos Chapman, Gavin Turk and Chris Ofili. And the Slade School of Art gave us Rachel Whiteread and Douglas Gordon, while Marc Quinn studied art history at Cambridge. Collectively, they become known as the YBAs – the Young British Artists[19].

The group is not bound by school or style in the manner of Abstract Expressionism or Pop Art. The YBAs comprised conceptually inclined painters, sculptors, photographers and installation artists, all with a penchant for shock and the grotesque. The group's primary characteristic, however, is a mere contingency, for it was their cultural milieu that gave them their distinct character. They lived in a desolate Britain on the cusp of great change: the 90s thrust Britain into the 21st century on a wave of new art (the YBAs), music (Britpop) and

---

[18] A brilliant account of the London art scene of the 1980s and its revolution throughout the 90s is given by Gregor Muir, *Lucky Kunst: The Rise and Fall of Young British Art* (London: Aurum Press, 2010).

[19] The term, 'YBA', has become unfashionable since the artists it denotes are no longer young. I insist on using it here as the name for an historically situated movement, which has nothing to do with age but everything to do with the emergence, from British art schools at a particular time in history, of a crop of artists who stood for a break with tradition and who would embed themselves in culture forever to be remembered as the Young British Artists regardless of how much they age.

politics (New Labour), all of which filled the dark hole left by recession and 18 years of Tory rule. The YBAs both capitalised upon and helped to create a new sense of hope.

Julian Stallabrass goes so far as to deny that the YBAs are bound by 'style and medium' and instead characterises the movement in terms of 'temperament and tactics'[20]. This bridges the considerable gap between Chris Ofili's paintings and Gillian Wearing's photographs or between Tracey Emin's installations and Damien Hirst's animals in formaldehyde. The temperament and tactics that neatly unites this diverse group of artists is characterised by the desire to shock in order to engage the audience and co-opt the mass media with a slick melding of high and low culture.

Furthermore, Stallabrass adds that a distinction of the YBAs is that they 'present conceptual work in visually accessible and spectacular form'[21], which sounds as if he is contradicting himself insofar as that is more a statement of style and medium than it is of temperament and tactics. Nonetheless, the visuality of conceptualism is a central tenet of that which made the YBAs both famous and great. Mass media, high/low culture, shock tactics, visual spectacle and conceptualism are the characteristics which unite the YBAs, even if they cannot be said to be a theoretically tight movement like the Abstract Expressionists or Pop Artists.

Stallabrass goes on to deny they are bound by an ideology, since the artists worked independently and entirely without a mutually agreed programme or manifesto like Surrealists, for instance. But it is worth pausing to critically unpick this claim. The YBAs were united in their promotion of

---

[20] Stallabrass, *High Art Lite,* revised and expanded edition (London: Verso, 2006), 3.
[21] Stallabrass, *High Art Lite,* 4.

the pervasive ideology of the 90s: at first it was an anti-establishment fight against the system that had wrecked the country and then later, with the arrival of Tony Blair, it became the neo-liberal ideology of freedom to pursue wealth and fame. The YBAs subscribed to both of these phases and the aesthetic they employed was a constant reflection of changing socio-economic conditions. In the early days, for example, Hirst made his cabinets from MDF and filled them with cigarette butts, whereas later he fashioned them from highly polished stainless steel and filled them with cubic zirconia. This move from the old Conservative recession art of the cheap and found to the New Labour era art boom of the expensive and manufactured is a reflection of the ideology of the art. It can be read in every facet of the YBAs' work from 1986 to 2000, as their materials, methods and ideas track the changes in national consciousness.

So, whilst this disparate group of artists may not have agreed a programme or an ideology, they were *a priori* bound up in a way of thinking and working in virtue of their being historically situated as they were. They were all living the anti-Tory pro-Labour ideology of the time, which culminated in the burning desire to make things better – to make everything and anything better in any way possible. The hubris of this ideology went so far that Blair's Labour party adopted D:Ream's song 'Things Can Only Get Better' as the anthem of their 1997 election campaign. The truly cringe-worthy thing is that it worked – everyone bought into it wholesale and Labour were elected on a landslide victory. The pervasive ideology of the time was thus one of improvement, reparation of past mistakes, restitution of happiness through aggressive modernisation and an abstract faith in the fullness of the future. As such, the art the YBAs made – individually and collectively – reflected that national unity of both the desire for change and a belief in its real possibility. Stallabrass is right that the YBAs did not explicitly agree on an ideology and write a manifesto, as the Surrealists did, but he is wrong to assume they did not thereby possess a collective ideology. It was, given the time and place, simply unavoidable.

The big historical claim here is that the YBAs laid the foundations for the artworld we now have, consisting of many galleries, even more artists, a vast market and an engaged general public. That is, they had a hand in creating the value industry itself. They did this in two ways: one, they made art popular, and two, they tied art to money; they peddled spectacle, consumerism, celebrity and popular culture on an industrial scale, creating value out of almost nothing and selling it to a positively famished art market. The concept of value shifted from the artist's technical skill to spectacle, a change that occurred at the level of public consciousness rather than in the purely theoretical core of art itself. Art became valuable insofar as it gained press attention, which powered sales. The value industry had been spawned – culture was marketed for profit, with minimal cost and effort, on the basis of inflated hearsay. Now that concept has dissipated into accepted normality, we are left with an artworld that is equally the wreckage of unregulated exuberance and the legacy of an inspired generation. It is owing to the very fact that YBAs unwittingly spawned the value industry, which embellishes the surface of contemporary art, that it is forgotten that that generation contained some of greatest British artists of the 20th Century, if not of all of art history.

The YBAs entered the scene in 1988 with 'Freeze', an exhibition of Goldsmiths' students curated and masterminded by Damien Hirst, which introduced, among other modern icons, Hirst's Spot Paintings. Over the course of three exhibitions in a disused warehouse in London's Docklands, the YBAs emerged as the most shocking, vital young artists around. There followed a string of group shows in the same vain, including 'Gambler' and 'Modern Medicine' (Building One, 1990), 'Young British Artists' (Saatchi Gallery, 1992-1996), 'Some Went Mad, Some Ran Away' (Serpentine Gallery, 1994) and 'Sensation' (Royal Academy, 1997). The YBAs had arrived and everyone in London was talking about it.

The calculated sensationalism drew a wide audience, while high-minded conceptualism and an historically entrenched aesthetic satisfied the establishment that it was the real deal. It was entrenched in the inescapable past, but stubbornly directed towards a bright future. Hirst's Medicine Cabinets fused the stark semantics of minimalism with a pop art interest in consumer culture. Gavin Turk tied history in knots, using the craft of waxworks to make a self-portrait as Sid Vicious dressed as Elvis. While Jake and Dinos Chapman took an anti-art, anti-aesthetic stance by mutilating an entire set of Goya's *Disasters of War* etchings with their trademark scribbles.

The YBAs were not intrinsically political, but they were products of their time and made art about the material conditions of life in an aesthetic language that was both simple and seductive. In the late 80s and early 90s, it felt as if contemporary art summed up the modern condition: Hirst's shark, *The Physical Impossibility of Death in the Mind of Someone Living* (1991), gave concrete form to the abstract fear of obliteration engendered by economic woe and the perennial threat of war, terror and nuclear fallout; Sarah Lucas' *Two Fried Eggs and a Kebab* (1994) and *Au Natural* (1994) captured the violence of gender stereotypes that was stirring in the wake of Margaret Thatcher's premiership; and Mark Wallinger's *Capital*

(1990), paintings of tramps in grand municipal settings, exposed the Thatcherite doting on the wealthy at the expense of the poor.

These messages might have fallen on deaf ears if it were not for their keen instinct for self-promotion and their ostentatious flirtation with the mass media. Enter Jay Jopling, owner of White Cube gallery, whose natural charm and gift for sales generated endless, lucrative publicity, leading to a memorable image in the *Daily Star* of a reporter posing with a bag of chips beside one of Hirst's fish cabinets. That was the scale of it – tabloid newspapers, normally concerned with cheating footballers and corrupt politicians, were splashing on art and artists. When Charles Saatchi first commissioned the shark from Hirst, it was reported in Britain's biggest tabloid, *The Sun*, with the headline '£50,000 for fish without chips'. The press watched the artists' every move with breathless anticipation, as the YBAs willingly became embroiled in the cult of celebrity.

The net result of this was that art became very popular indeed: people flocked to galleries and museums, and talked about the exciting new art and its celebrity protagonists as if it mattered – even people who had never before professed or pursued any interest in art. While this is partly due to the work itself, it is also due to the seduction of celebrity. By throwing themselves into the media spotlight the YBAs made art a popular pastime, and the effect has been that the Tate, for example, is able to have blockbuster shows that appeal to a general audience and contemporary art is sufficiently enmeshed in public consciousness that it has an abiding media presence.

Aside from the shocking new art and their A-list hijinks, the YBAs became famous for the money. Owing to a few wealthy collectors at first and then a rejuvenated economy, ever-increasing sums of money changed hands, and staggering numbers always make good headlines. When, in 1991, Saatchi paid £50,000 for Hirst's shark, it was an indecent sum of money for a work by a largely unknown artist (and remains so now). So, something had gone very right indeed when Saatchi sold it in 2004 to American hedge-fund manager Steven A Cohen for an alleged $12,000,000[22] – at the time the highest price for a work by a living artist other than Jasper Johns. For Hirst, the first work to sell for £1,000,000 was *Hymn*, bought by Saatchi in 2000. Prior to that, prices had been steadily creeping up; after that they rocketed year on year. Hirst made £11,000,000 in 2003 from his sell-out show, 'Romance in the Age of Uncertainty', at White Cube; £50,000,000 in 2007 for the infamous diamond skill, *For the Love of God*; and bypassed his dealers to sell 223 lots at Sotheby's in 2008 for £111,000,000. It worked in much the same way for the others, particularly Emin: Saatchi bought Emin's *My Bed* (1998) for £150,000 in 2000 and sold it in 2014 for slightly more than £2,500,000[23].

The chance meeting of three individuals, Damien Hirst, Jay Jopling and Charles Saatchi, formed a holy trinity of the manufacturer, the seller and the consumer. Hirst's seemingly unstoppable genius, Jopling's exemplary salesmanship and Saatchi's insatiable desire signalled to the international art market that London was ready, willing and able to join in. The art market is self-perpetuating: once there is someone like Saatchi buying so much, everyone else starts to think they are

---

[22] The precise figure is unknown. Some reports say it was $8,000,000, but the widely-held figure of $12,000,000 has been greatly popularised by Don Thompson, *The $12 Million Stuffed Shark: The Curious Economics of the Contemporary Art Market* (London: Aurum Press, 2012).

[23] See Chapter 5, Everything You Steel Will Turn to Ash, for more on this.

missing out if they too are not buying the same stuff. And once the demand rises, things either became scarce, and therefore expensive, or, as with Hirst, production is stepped up accordingly and prises rise anyway, just because people will pay. And thus was spawned a market that eventually grew so strong that it could defy even global financial meltdown.

All this created the kind of market confidence that brought big blue-chip galleries to London. The more the YBAs sold, the more collectors wanted, and the more the international artworld wanted a slice of the action. Eventually – with the help of an improving economy – it led to today's multiplication of commercial galleries, which can only survive because the YBAs helped create a climate in which art is a necessary luxury for the wealthy. Furthermore, since art was so popular, market confidence created the conditions for smaller, more modestly priced, galleries to open so now there is something for everyone who wants it.

The YBAs created economic value, in terms of their personal wealth and the market's value, but they also created enduring cultural value in terms of the value of art to society and the value of their work in and of itself. But perhaps more importantly, they filled the welter left behind by a poverty of both art and politics, creating a miraculous situation that today we almost take for granted: a climate in which art is popular, accessible and even necessary to the core of British society.

The paradox is that the YBAs fought the Establishment, only to become the Establishment themselves and thus created a bigger, more money-soaked Establishment than that which existed before. But that, as with all stories of progress, is par for the course and does not dent the world of possibilities that the new world order allows. And the new world order is that of the value industry: the YBAs created value out of the nothingness at their immediate disposal, which became the blueprint for contemporary art the world over ever since, and which enabled that wayward boy from Leeds to buy everything he ever wanted, including a very big house in the country…

Spot the Difference

The distinction between cultural and economic value is central to understanding the relationship between art and money because art possesses these two values simultaneously and necessarily. A concrete example of the distinction should help to flesh out exactly how it works in practice. We will begin with the exception rather than the rule – an example of where economic value follows from cultural value in such a way that one would be forgiven for thinking their relationship is entirely reciprocal.

The first 1,365 of Damien Hirst's infamous Spot Paintings are chronicled in a catalogue raisonné, *The Complete Spot Paintings 1986-2011*[24]. It was published following an exhibition of the same name, in 2012, that occurred simultaneously in all eleven international branches of Gagosian Gallery[25]. The exhibition featured 300 Spot Paintings of all sizes and colours, and aimed to illustrate how the same thing is always more different than you think. The catalogue was supposed to bolster market confidence in the series by proving that the notorious paintings are less numerous than rumoured. But the value of a Spot Painting is about so much more than

[24] *Damien Hirst: The Complete Spot Paintings 1986-2011*, ed. Michael Bracewell (London and New York: Other Criteria and Gagosian, 2013).
[25] Damien Hirst, 'The Complete Spot Paintings 1986-2011", Gagosian Gallery London, New York, Paris, Athens, Geneva, Los Angeles and Rome.

how many there are: it is a matter of seeing a given Spot Painting as a unique artwork which has a place in both a series of works and in an art historical narrative.

The beauty of the Spot Paintings resides in the conceptual economy of the fact that their entire meaning is perfectly expressed by a few simple rules of production: the gaps between spots must be equal to the size of the spots, no colour is repeated on a single canvas, and they are to be named according to categories, such as pharmaceuticals, determined by the colour pallet[26]. This formula can be repeated and realised forever. And that pure mathematical infinity expresses the immortality of the Spot Painting series, which in turn expresses the delusion of immortality promised by the pharmaceuticals after which many of them – the original series, at least – are named. In other words, owing to this simple formula, different Spot Paintings can continue to be made so long as death continues to occur.

How, then, do we value something so numerous? It might be thought that the sheer proliferation of Spot Paintings devalues them, as if owning one is tantamount to owning any other. But this could not be further from reality. It could only be the case if we refuse to recognise that each Spot Painting is a unique work of art, aesthetically different from all the others with which it shares a common conceptual connection. So although we may pretheoretically think that all Spot Paintings are the same, they are, in fact, aesthetically different from one

---

[26] The Spot Paintings with which we are most familiar come from the 'Pharmaceutical' series, which is only one of fourteen sub-categories of Spot Paintings. The same rules about spot size and spacing apply to most of the other categories, but each category is differentiated by a distinct colour scheme. Furthermore, categories are denoted by titles, such as 'Venoms' or 'Carbon-13 Labelled Compounds', which dictate the names of individual works within the category.

another, and are therefore aesthetically distinct works of art. Value, then, is to be discerned in their individuality, and not in their infamous plurality.

Consider *Edge* (1988) and *Row* (1988): both are painted directly onto the wall, both with the same size spots, both with the same colour sequence and so both visually very similar. The devil is in the detail: in *Edge*, the last column of spots is cut in half on the right-hand side, whereas in *Row* the last row of spots is halved along the bottom. It is often in this subtlety of detail that the differences between Spot Paintings resides. Now compare these to *L-Leucine 15-N* (2001), 12 metres wide with 4-inch coloured spots, or even *Chlorobenzene* (2002), a circular canvas with greyscale spots: here you witness radical departures from everything that *Edge* and *Row*, and indeed most other Spot Paintings you have ever seen, have given you to believe. So when we say there are 1,365 Spot Paintings, we are making two distinct claims: one, the conceptual claim that are there so many iterations of the formula; and two, the aesthetic claim that there are individual, finitely differentiated artworks.

It should be apparent by now that the Spot Paintings depend on both the aesthetic and the conceptual claim in order to make sense. That is, the very fact that the conceptual claim holds in all cases validates the aesthetic claim. Now we can see that the number of Spot Paintings plays a different role in determining value from that which we originally thought. Rather than the value decreasing due to the number of paintings in existence, we can now see that value is primarily determined by the fact that each painting is aesthetically different from the next. Rather than recognise this aesthetic fact, however, the market currently takes a pseudo-historical approach by attaching higher prices to older works, as if the whole of history had been sped up and an early 90s Spot Painting has the lofty status of a relic.

The better approach, however, is to explore how cultural and economic value are created by the conceptual and aesthetic components of the paintings. We might thus view the Spot Paintings as unique artworks with differential cultural values, which in turn determines their economic values. Graw argues that although a high price does not guarantee the work is culturally valuable, the right critical response to a work can bolster its economic value[27]. On this model, the economic value of a given Spot Painting is determined by its cultural value, which is determined by the uniqueness of the work as it is situated within a conceptually rule-governed series. Here, 'uniqueness' will be a matter of degrees, defined by how many works in the series are more or less aesthetically similar to a given work. For example, as the majority of the works, the Pharmaceutical paintings are the least unique overall, so any given one is culturally less valuable than one from another series, such as Carbon 13-Labelled Compounds, because it aesthetically resembles many others. However, the Sedative series of paintings (with only greyscale spots) is a much smaller group, so any given painting therein will be more aesthetically unique in the overall category of Spot Paintings.

The point here is to demonstrate that when we talk about 'cultural value', we are not talking about something abstract or theoretical. Rather, cultural value is a judgement we make of art all the time; it is a judgement of value based on the aesthetic (that this, the things we see and experience) and conceptual (ideas, meanings, theoretical) content of the artwork; it is a judgement of the worth – to culture, history and peoples – of the work of art, and therefore of how far we

---

[27] See Graw, *High Price*, Chapter 1.

reasonably expect it to endure through time and the contribution it makes to culture. This is a value judgement in its purest form because we ultimately use it to decree the work good or bad or worthwhile or whatever. As such, it determines, at least in part, economic value, for what an artwork is worth on the open market is – implicitly, at least – a judgement of how good or worthy it is.

For example, an early or mid-career Picasso painting, which epitomises cubism, can set you back anywhere up to around $100,000,000, but you can get your hands on a late Picasso, from the 1970s, for between $2,000,000 and 4,000,000. The difference in price – in economic value – is simply a difference in cultural value: the later Picassos are regarded as tired, washed out and lacking in the artist's youthful energy and signature flourish. In short, they are relatively cheap because they are thought to be (relatively) not very good. This is a coarse conception of value which, remember, is here the exception rather than the rule[28].

The same thing applies to the Spot Paintings: it is possible for there to be good ones and bad ones, aesthetically speaking, because each one is unique, which means they will have differing cultural values that therefore determine different economic values. Cultural and economic value are the two spirits behind the mystery of art prices, and once we see how they are interlinked and how they determine price, the price of art begins to make sense. The cultural value of the Spot Paintings, then, resides in their aesthetic qualities, which should be largely unsurprising. The more surprising fact is that – owing to the aesthetic qualities and conceptual content of

---

[28] Later on, we shall see young artists who are priced according to fashion rather than aesthetics (Chapter 2), highly bankable celebrities who make worthless art (Chapter 6), and expensive but not very interesting Richters (Chapter 7)

the series – works with greater cultural value will therefore have a greater economic value.

Another thing that starts to emerge, which we should treat at this stage with extreme caution, is that value (insofar as it is cultural) plays a direct, positive role in price. So far, we have considered cases where higher prices are offered for works which reasonably have a higher cultural value in virtue of their superior aesthetic (and/or conceptual) qualities; as such, here cultural value contributes in a meaningful way to economic value. Whilst this is correct for some cases, it cannot be the whole story, since we know intuitively that all artworks are not sold for a fair, correct or reasonable price. Some works, we know, are overpriced, especially when we consider their aesthetic and conceptual qualities to be somewhat lacking and therefore undeserving of the price. There must be something else going on. That something else, we shall see in due course, is the power of mythologies, which artificially inflate prices where the work is otherwise deficient.

Nonetheless, in the case of the Spot Paintings, cultural and economic value coincide rather neatly and accurately: they are attractive, simple, elegant and regular enough to be conceptually coherent but varied enough to allow for surprises. The most valuable ones will thus be the ones that are most different from the others because they possess an aesthetic and/or conceptual distinction from their brethren.

One consequence of this is that value will be determined by extreme deviation from the rule: when everything looks so similar, the ones that stand out are the ones that brazenly flout the conceptual rule, such as *Mickey Mouse* (2012), a portrait of the Disney character, and *Iopanoic Acid* (2011), a depiction of Ronnie O'Sullivan's fastest ever 147 break. These works have a higher cultural value because they are simultaneously part of the series and they transcend the rules about spacing and size of spots and the non-repetition of colour. As the most exceptional, they have the highest cultural, and therefore economic, value of all the series. There are others that similarly break the rules in different ways, but, out of a series of 1,365 paintings, they remain the minority.

In more general terms, the cultural value of the Spot Paintings resides in their position as seminal works of the – at the time – ground-breaking YBA movement. The Spot Paintings hailed a period of art history in which reproducibility and repetition were more important than uniqueness, and became icons of their time. Like them or not, they will be remembered as monuments of the 90s and their contribution to culture is precisely as such, for to own a Spot Painting is to own a slice of history, a revolutionary icon which reveals the owner to be a mover or shaker. The value of culture is, after all, the extent to which it enriches human life and encourages flourishing – and these grids of coloured dots did just that at a time when it was abundantly necessary, so to own one of those is to be associated with that rich cultural heritage.

The fact that the deviant Spot Paintings differ so markedly from the standard is precisely what makes them desirable cultural products. Indeed, the entire series is sustained by these deviations because any respectable collection of Spot Paintings would want to include one of them. Here is an example of economic value following cultural value in quite a rigid and, as it happens, predictable manner, and although we shall see other examples of this, they will be less clear-cut than this one. In the forgoing chapters, we shall see the connection between the two kinds of value to be more fluid, since very often prices reflect something other than cultural value, or they are otherwise out of synch with it.

II. The Expensive and the Good

The relationship between price and quality

It will come as no surprise that economic value does not necessarily denote good quality, nor must it follow from positive cultural value; it only has to be justifiable by any means available to hand. It is, after all, the business of the value industry to create value wherever and however it can. The market, on its inexorable whim, sometimes constructs economic value on the basis of fashion rather than an appreciation of aesthetics. In these cases, economic value is established before the artworld has had an opportunity to soberly confer a judgement of cultural value. Consequently, cultural and economic value are out of sync: the latter is prior to the former, and yet the high prices create the illusion that cultural value has been assured.

The Simulacrum of Success

Consider, first, how economic value can be established with some certainty even before any notion of cultural value has been assured. Around about 2011, a slew of young artists began to realise staggeringly high prices at auction, demonstrating the perennial muddle of price and quality, where buyers' spending habits were confused with judgements of artistic worth.

The trend for young, relatively unknown artists fetching surprising prices began with American painter, Jacob Kassay. At the age of 28, he commanded six figure sums at auction with a series of remarkably clever paintings which captured the imaginations of buyers who conflate bling with beauty. Kassay made shiny paintings with a unique chemical process, priming the canvas with acrylic, saturating it with chemicals, adding a layer of silver deposit and burning the edges. The result was an effect of ghostly translucence, a foggy mirror that manages only a partial reflection[29].

In May 2011, Kassay's paintings were selling at Philips, New York, for a respectable $30,000, but by November that year they had rocketed to $206,500. Kassay's prices had risen according to the law of artworld chatter: talk the right talk to the right people and the resultant hubris drives prices skyward. In addition to his performance in the saleroom – or perhaps, as a result of it – on the other side of the Atlantic, Kassay was involved in two major events in London. First, he was in the group show, 'Structure and Absence', which inaugurated White Cube's monumental Bermondsey space; and second, he staged

---

[29] Kassay has long since moved on from these works, abandoning a lucrative series very much to his credit.

a solo show at London's prestigious Institute of Contemporary Art, known for its championing of emerging talent[30].

This is how careers are made in the artworld: arbitrarily, by sleight of hand of the market, with less focus on the work than on the amount of hoo-ha it can generate. So it goes in art. The market is the engine which powers the reputation machine, leading the world to think that prices denote quality. In truth, Kassay's paintings are clever and pretty, but they are not – in the grand scheme of monochrome abstract painting – earth-shattering. He is no Barnet Newman or Mark Rothko, for once the awe of the works' initial appearance has subsided, they have nothing more to give; there is no shifting focus of form, no existential mystery, just a plane of pigment that depends for all its majesty on an insidious trick. Great paintings give you more over time, but Kassay's eventually fizzle into a welter of sameness. The silver mirror paintings are not great painting, although they are exemplary trendy loft-apartment decoration.

The same happened with Oscar Murillo, tellingly represented by David Zwirner. Murillo's messy paintings, which affect an awkward fusion of a poor-man's Basquiat with Latin American youth culture, sold comfortably at Christie's for £192,000. They were so popular for a time that Kenny Schachter, the most honest man in the artworld, quipped that every Murillo ever made had changed hands at least once. Such is the market – the buzz of speculation leads to constant exchange. Murillo is not without artistic merit, but his market was driven by fashion: in the absence of the possibility of new, fresh Basquiats – an auction favourite – Murillo was hailed as the second-coming, which chimed with a burgeoning fascination with street art. Murillo's market was based on a

---

[30] Both events occurred in October 2011.

romantic notion of art that was a product of the street, of the Other world outside of the gallery, which spoke a language that intellectual or historically entrenched painting could not master. He was in the right place at the right time with the right paintings, and the market found it irresistible.

In the case of both Kassay and Murillo, economic value was taken to assure cultural value; that is, the price itself, and the fact it grew steadily, was taken to denote a superior quality. The danger here is clear to see if we remove the rose-tinted glasses of market success. These artists, enjoying the convincing simulacrum of artistic success, are driven to mass-produce the works which buyers queue up to get hold of only to sell them on again a year later, as if an endless journey through the market equates to posterity. But they lacked the solid critical foundation on which their work could be taken seriously as art rather than as commodity simply because they had not been around for long enough for the work to be studied and appraised.

These artists were making work which spoke to the zeitgeist of the market, which fulfilled a need in the culture and a gap in the collectors' sense of their own trendiness, but did nothing to resonate with the wider socio-historical epoch of their making. Kassay and Murillo were on the right side of the aesthetic favoured by buyers, but not necessarily on the right side of the living heat of art history: the former, a stark, cool, glitzy loft-apartment minimalism, and the latter, a politicised, energetic, youthful street vibe. On the one hand, a pristine, clean-cut boy from New York State, on the other hand, an edgy, self-aware lad from Columbia. They were the stuff of dreams.

The market might sometimes be a reliable taste-maker, but it is not thereby a guarantor of aesthetic quality. The

Kassay paintings are high fashion for a low art audience who wants to muscle in on the trendy nowness of contemporary art, but that kind of 'clever', faux-scientific painting goes through phases of popularity. Murillo was stuck like a leach to the more recent and more instantly cool idea – rather than the concrete reality – of street art. The artworld supposed it promised a renewed political consciousness that could engage art with the difficulties of the 21st Century. It also thought of the street as a sort of conceptual Other to the gallery, where white cubes are replaced by gritty scenes of discontent and an alarming but exhilarating contingency. The net result in both cases is an immaculate conception of fashion, but a short-sightedness in terms of real cultural longevity – while both artists have their merits, there is nothing aesthetically convincing in the work, such that Kassay is a poor man's abstract expressionist and Murillo is a budget Basquiat.

The market sold the work on the basis of an all-encompassing popularity contest. It is difficult not to notice that, whilst there are plenty of such artists just out of school, the ones pounced upon by the market happen to be well-educated, ultra-fashionable, malleable young men who have enough personality and artistic prowess to sell, but not so much as to make grand promises about the future. The artworld latched on to style over substance, but never did the intellectual groundwork to ensure cultural value would outlive the transient economic value. Now, those once ubiquitous Kassays and Murillos are a distant memory, rarely seen and rarely sold, which is a consequence of their economic value being rashly considered without due care and attention to cultural value. The value industry, in the final analysis, cares about fashion because fashion sells, which, in this case, has nothing whatever to do with the quality of what is being sold.

Peake Performance

In contrast to Kassay and Murillo, there are occasions when a young, fashionable artist establishes the cultural value of their work long before it has attained any noteworthy economic value. Eddie Peake, a bright star twinkling in the infernal blackness that traverses the space between economics and culture, made his auction début at Christie's in February 2014. On that occasion, he sold one of his mirror paintings, which realised £32,000 (more than double its high estimate), but this was only after he had toiled at developing an intellectually informed practice that gave critics pause and caused markets to act initially with caution.

Peake is diverse and complex, for no matter how he performs in the market, a great deal of criticism is needed to work out what his beguiling work is all about. At first glance, Peake seems to fit the mould of trendy young artists: he is good-looking, well-connected to all the art people about town, and he makes work which speaks in a multi-layered way to the zeitgeist; his practice includes performance, sculpture and painting, enacting a unique fusion of theatrics and objects that both glitter like gold and embody the word on the street. It is like the bling of Kassay with the edge of Murillo, but with a slow-burning intelligence, and this rising star established the quality of his work on the cultural platform as a precursor to the prices.

Born in London in 1981, Peake graduated from the Slade in 2006, before taking up a residency at the prestigious British School in Rome in 2008. While at the Royal Academy Schools, he staged *Touch* (2012), a naked five-a-side football match, which got the chattering classes chattering, leading to a performance to open Tate Modern's Tanks with the hilariously titled *Amidst a Sea of Flailing High Heels and Cooking Utensils* (2012). Then he exhibited 'Adjective Machine Gun' (2013) at White Cube Bermondsey, which gained him full representation by the gallery.

In addition to performance, Peake has a stable of three-dimensional works, including his series of delicious mirror paintings: highly polished steel with lacquered spray paint applied to create slogans in the parlance of his native North London: they say funny, awkward things like 'hard dick in batty', 'crushingly hopeless' and 'he doesn't need to know'. These pieces slot neatly into a certain trend for street art, but with an intoxicating, irresistible, seductive high art finish; they possess a distinct visual language and they look magical on the wall. They are certainly very sellable, but they are also unsettlingly enchanting in the way that they feed on the viewer's changing mood for their constant fluctuations in meaning: at one moment they are mirrors and at another they are posters, and at all moments they are both, so it really depends upon one's momentary disposition whether one feels attacked by or indifferent to their provocative slogans.

Touch, where the teams are differentiated only by the colours of their socks, perfectly illustrates why Peake is a serious, talented artist. He casts the audience as voyeurs whose gaze oscillates awkwardly between eroticism and artistry: the male form is presented as object of desire and as pure sculptural entity. The audience, in Peake's work, is always thus participant rather than passive receiver; it creates the performance by looking, by gazing, thinking, judging, responding, which develops the semantic content of the work. The performance is an intellectual provocation and it is a bunch of lads playing sport; the movements are instinctive, natural and alluring, and they are choreographed into high art ballet. At the end, you feel delicately ashamed of your voyeurism. Peake has orchestrated it in such a way that it possesses the discrete charm of an ambiguous joke: it is more than gratuitous nudity because it is deliberately poetic, but it is somehow less than the neutrality of the Nude because the physical form of the performers is part of the spectacle.

It has been said that Peake's work is homoerotic, but this is a gloss on the crude fact that it consists in a boy getting other boys to take their clothes off. Homoeroticism would comprise, first, its being primarily aimed at men, and second, an attempt to elicit a response of desire. Neither of these especially apply to Peake's work. In essence, homoeroticism is a simple-minded attempt at stirring mischievous excitement, but Peake's work is infinitely more complex, even if it does consciously play on those key elements. Moreover, there is no plausible sense in which Peake is aiming at a predominantly male audience, so any claim of homoeroticism dissolves on closer inspection. There is no doubt that it is supposed to be erotic *on some level* but where that is directed remains an open question. Gay men may find *Touch* sexually interesting, as might straight women, but frankly, who knows what straight men think of it – and this is not to consider the numerous nuances of gender and sexuality in between. In the end, insofar as eroticism and desire are concerned, perhaps Peake's point is precisely that aesthetic responses to the naked body cannot any longer be sensibly or plausibly codified by binary concepts of gender and sexuality.

Peake occupies a liminal space where the gaze, or the Sartrean Look, is confounded: whilst you are looking at the Other, you are never sure what you are supposed to be looking at – a football match, a work of art, or a group of naked men, which are conceptually very different things. And you are never sure what you are supposed to be looking for: whilst you are assured there is an intellectual point, it fizzles somewhere just out of reach, as if you are confronted with the entirely erroneous task of viewing pornography as art or ballet as pornography. The only certainty is that you should be looking – there is a spectacle occurring and it is trying to tell you something.

On seeing the mirror paintings and the performance together at White Cube, it became clear that Peake is engaged in an extraordinarily refined socio-political critique. Moving around the gallery, that confusing eroticism crept out of every encounter, no matter how seemingly innocent and ordinary. The exhibition was punctuated by the movements of a young man on roller-skates, whose sole duty was to roll at speed across the polished concrete floors and strike a pose. The roller-skater's body was enhanced and foregrounded by his tight-fitting, translucent boiler suit, leaving nothing to the imagination, which created a tension between the paintings and the performance. On the one hand, you found yourself in the midst of motion, the soft grating whirl of roller-skates on concrete, the swift, agile movements of the man and his classical, almost unselfconsciously nonchalant poses. But on the other hand, you found yourself gripped by stillness, staring deep into the lacquered surfaces of the paintings where paint and steel are forever fixed in their predetermined form. As you looked at the paintings, pulling your best quizzical art face, half your attention was detained by the roller-skater – his form and motion irresistible. Then you caught your guilty reflection in one of the mirror paintings. You were outwardly looking at art, but inwardly you were doing something else entirely – no matter whether your response to the thinly veiled male nude was one of thrill or shrill, you were a willing voyeur of

Daniel Barnes

someone else's body. The fact that the paintings were concurrent with the performance only muddied the waters still further, for it became a chicken and egg scenario – did the paintings occasion the voyeurism with their reflective surfaces, or did the voyeurism come first with the paintings as the guardian of decency?

But therein lies Peake's ingenious conceit: not only do you study the painting in the intended manner, you see yourself, as if catching yourself in the act. No matter whether you perceived intended eroticism, you became the subject and object exactly at the moment you were trying to behave as if the object before you and the subject skating around you were entirely unconnected. In a crushing instant you realise that this work is trying to make you look in on yourself as the constant, unflinching voyeur. It is not about them at all, it is all about you and what you are doing whilst these nice boys are going about the business that the gallery has paid them to do. Peake lures you in with the promise of *jouissace* in the Other and then turns it back on you, causing the edifice of your high-minded artworld pretence to crumble into a severe questioning of a society which encourages us to just look at things.

It is this complexity, this uncertainty and this intellectual prowess that eventually made Peake a market success. The work wears its cultural value on its sleeve with its fusion of performance and desirable objects that gather in together so many art historical traditions and then confound them all. Peake appeals to the zeitgeist and then turns it on its head by doing something that is difficult, although not impossible, to grasp, which sent critics raving so the saleroom could not resist.

But market success is only telling half the story – the bit about the highly desirable objects – whereas the magic of

Peake is in the transcendent wonder of the totality. The Peake package that the market is selling is the same old bundle of trendy treasures, but that is eclipsed by the fact they are part of a razor-sharp critique of contemporary society, rendered in an aesthetic that is very Now and very Tomorrow. So when that mirror painting sold at Christie's in 2014 for more than double its high estimate, it was the culmination of years of critical manoeuvring. Here we see economic value following logically and dutifully from critical acclaim, reflecting the way in which the market sometimes has no choice but to follow in the footsteps of culture. Testament to Peake's integrity and intelligence, he was still doing the same thing – melding performance with painting and sculpture – more than half a decade after his first White Cube show. It is that commitment to ideas and aesthetics, and, to an extent, resilience to the allure of the market, that will, all things being equal, ensure a long and rich career for Peake.

Total Eclipse of the Art

Buying art as an investment tends to seem like a good idea because, unlike stocks or shares, the prices never go down. The rewards are not just financial, for in buying a work of art, a person is exercising their judgement of taste, which makes them feel refined and cultured. And in selling it on, they have that refined taste confirmed not just by the fact that someone wants to buy it, but also by their confidence in the product inherent in the price they are willing to pay for it.

But in the case of fakes chaos unfolds: the market's intractable rule is momentarily suspended and, as if under emergency law, it has to allow prices to go down. In these cases, the cultural value and the price of an artwork match each other exactly like a solar eclipse, where an inflated dealer's head blocks out all the light emanating from the knowledge of an expert. An example of this occurred in the UK on a BBC1 television programme in the revelation of a fake Marc Chagall painting. Owning a fake artwork is devastating for the collector and embarrassing for the dealer, but it is nothing but good news for the integrity of art, and in this case, it offers a splendid display of draconian ethics applied to cultural production.

In the early 90s, a businessman named Martin Lang bought Chagall's *Nude 1909-10* for £100,000. A Chagall does not need a price-tag to guarantee its cultural value, for history has seen to it that, although there is a sliding scale of important to minor works, a Chagall is valuable *as* a Chagall. In this case, the modest price reflected it being a minor work, but also a lingering doubt over the painting's authenticity, which must have been sufficiently minimal and untroublesome in the mind of both dealer and buyer to enable the transaction to go ahead.

Chagall's estate is centrally managed by the Chagall Commission in Paris, but owing to his dual heritage, the Russians have a hand in proffering pronouncements on authenticity. This particular painting was purchased from a Russian dealer who waved the wand of authentication on the basis of the picture's appearance in a Soviet catalogue. Lang bought the work with the intention of first, verifying its authenticity and second, holding on to it as an investment to be sold at retirement.

It all went wrong twenty-two years later, when Lang began to think about selling the painting. A genuine Chagall of that quality could sell for £500,000, even though, having held on to it and watched the crash-proof market sell Chagalls for

$10,000,000, Lang dreamt of rather more. One would think that on the advice of an expert and with the attachment one fosters over so many years Lang was sure in his conviction of the work's authenticity. It was a brush with the normally insipid arts team at the BBC that dramatically changed his fortunes: in a last bid to eschew any doubt, Lang featured the work in the programme *Fake or Fortune?*[31]. Scrutiny proved it to be a fake, dashing all hope of a fortune, demolishing years of pride and subtracting an artefact from the Chagall corpus.

The next part of the story is nothing short of breathtaking: the Chagall Committee decided to enact an archaic French law which requires the painting to be extradited to France and burnt in a courtroom in front of a judge because forgery, so it goes, is both an artistic crime and an economic crime. There are two things going on here: one, the painting was judged worthless *as a Chagall*; and two, it is worthless *as a painting,* regardless of who made it. Lang, who parted with £100,000 for the artefact, understandably fought to keep the painting precisely because it was still a painting by somebody (that is, a work of art), but the Chagall committee were adamant that if it was not the Chagall it claimed to be, then it was a worthless affront. The painting enacts a dual transgression – it commits the artistic crime of pretending to be something it is not, and it commits the economic crime of profiting from a lie. As far as the Chagall Committee was concerned, the painting had zero value: it had no economic value precisely because it had no cultural value. But things are not as clear-cut as the Committee's response suggests.

There is a sense in which we may be willing to forgive the artistic crime, which was aided and abetted by the initial authenticator, because after the storm has blown over the

---

[31] Broadcast on Sunday 2 February 2014, BBC1.

painting is still a work of art, made by an artist, which in itself possesses the core values of art. It is, after all, a painting situated within an art historical tradition, which has an aesthetic of its own and is therefore valuable to some degree as such. It is interesting, then, that the Chagall Committee took such a harsh line, saying that since the work was not what it claimed to be, then it is worthless; a position which clearly privileges the artistic crime above all other concerns.

Those opposed to the destruction of the painting will cite the fact that it is still the fruit of someone's artistic labour and that it was purchased by someone for a monetary value. After all, as an object on the market, it must have *some* economic value. This position clearly holds sway for Lang, the purchaser of this fruit of artistic labour, but does little to confer economic value because the identity of that artist is unknown and is somewhat mitigated by the moral fact that the artist's intention was less to produce a painting than it was to deceive. That is, if the painting is worth anything at all as a mere painting, then it is worth very little indeed as anything at all.

Ultimately, the Committee was right to dismiss the work as utterly worthless. On a moral level, an example should be set to those who wish to defame the names of great artists and deceive collectors. But on a cultural level, more importantly, the collision of cultural and economic value is rare and when it occurs it preserves the integrity of an art market that is otherwise constantly viewed with suspicion. The important thing about the work – equally in the eyes of the painter, the seller and the buyer – is that it purports to be a Chagall; indeed, this is and was the only reason for its existence in the first place. Therefore, it claims to have an aesthetic and a history, an aura, if you like, that it simply does not possess; without all that it is just another painting, like many millions of others, whose value resides only in the most casual and fleeting association with what it is to be a work of art. But given the spurious claim to have been a Chagall, cultural and economic value suddenly coincide, ending in a zero-sum game for all: it has no value as a Chagall because it is not one, and it has no value as a painting because it is less an attempt at aesthetics and more an attempt at deception; therefore, the economic value of zero perfectly matches the null cultural value. Just as a solar eclipse provides a haunting moment of calm in the chaos of the skies, fakes provide an opportunity to reflect on the rampant bustle of an artworld that seems so at odds with aesthetics and yet sometimes makes the right judgement call on value.

Bringing Home the Bacon

In the same way that a fake is justifiably deemed to be worthless, there are occasions when an astronomical price is fair and reasonable because, as Graw says, the art market is putting a price on that which is priceless. Here we will consider a case in which it is difficult for economic value to truly reflect cultural value because the artist is perceived to have achieved such a lofty status that practically no price is too high. Nonetheless, the economic value which the work ends up with is just about as good a match as there ever could be for the work's cultural value.

The cultural value of art, as we have seen, consists in its propensity to affect those people who come in to contact with it. Art is valuable to us precisely because it has the power to move us emotionally and intellectually; it expresses feelings, offers existential insight and even fosters social agitation. We commune with works of art on all manner of levels and we regard this as a worthy – even essential – part of the fabric of life. This is foremost in the individual's commerce with art, which, although it sounds rather evangelical, is intrinsic to the flourishing of the human spirit. Of course, you might say you cannot put a price on that, but in the age of global capitalism everything has a price.

Museums will often stretch their finances to acquire a work precisely because it is their job to secure for the people the possibility of that unique edification of the spirit. For example, London's National Gallery scrimped and saved to pay £45,000,000 for Titian's *Diana and Callisto* (1556-69)[32]. That, it seems, is the price of great art. Similarly, Francis Bacon's *Portrait of George Dyer Talking* (1966) sold at Christie's London for £42,194,500[33]. It does not seem to be a complete coincidence that the Titian cost about the same amount as the Bacon, as we shall see in a moment, but first we should wonder whether a painting could ever really be worth that much money.

We are not speaking here of the price of a mere object or a commodity in the system of consumerism, nor even the price of an historic relic. It is the monetary value attached to the esteem in which we, and successive generations, hold a work of art. In the case of Bacon's *Portrait of George Dyer Talking*, the price realised is partly a reflection of an individual's judgement of *artistic* value, which combines historical importance with aesthetic judgement. It is also an acknowledgement of that fact that it possesses the capacity to move the viewer in a way that is rare in most works of art, which applies equally to the Titian.

---

[32] Bought by the National Gallery in 2012.
[33] 13 February 2014.

In both cases, this mysterious capacity contributes to the justification of the price.

This capacity is rather distinct but difficult to characterise because it is a viewer's response to the qualities of the work; nonetheless, it is a response that we can reasonably expect most people to have. The philosopher Immanuel Kant might help us here: Kant developed the notion of the sublime, which is the sense of awe and wonder we feel when faced with something – a mountain range, a sunset, a painting – that is extraordinarily complex and/or very large. As Kant says, 'We call that sublime which is absolutely great'[34], and this greatness, for Kant, is characterised by its being 'boundless', which only means, for our purposes, that the greatness we perceive is partially a result of something external to the object. In the case of painting, this would be the viewer's perceptions, thoughts, prejudices, knowledge of art history and the like, which entail the meaning or effect of the painting is boundless because it depends upon the viewer's interpretation, which cannot be limited or bounded in advance of any given viewer perceiving the work[35].

The awe we feel is a result of both our understanding that the thing is made of many distinct parts, which individually we understand even if we do not understand their totality, and a kind of amazement at the sheer bulk of it. For example, we have this feeling in the face of mountain ranges because although we may understand the discrete concepts of rock formations and landscapes, we cannot conceive of their

---

[34] Immanuel Kant, *Critique of Judgement*, trans. JH Bernard (London: Macmillan, 1951), § 25.

[35] Kant distinguishes between the dynamical sublime for things that are complex and the mathematical sublime for things that are large. For our purpose, this distinction does not matter, for we are interested in conceptualising the notion of greatness.

conglomeration in such massive and complex arrangements. Similarly, while we may understand the ideas of colour and form, Titian's *Diana and Callisto* brings them together with such subtlety and complexity that we are dumbfounded and amazed in its presence. This feeling of greatness varies from person to person but Kant would hold that everyone who engages with the object should feel it to some extent or another, which is precisely what we tend to think about great works of art, and this is precisely how we arrive at a seemingly universal notion of cultural value. You can deny Titian, but you cannot doubt a certain greatness of effect in his pictures. It is this, the fact that everyone should agree on a certain base level of aesthetic judgements, that Kant is getting at. We might call this particular aesthetic response to artworks 'reverence', for it is precisely that sense of majesty and greatness that some works inspire, causing them to be revered the world over. Insofar as the art market is ever consciously trading on cultural value, it is often this reverence that inspires and justifies the prices of Bacons and Titians. So, given their fairly equal reverence, it is not a coincidence that they end up with about the same price.

This demonstrates that once cultural value has been established beyond doubt, economic value must reflect it, so that prices cannot in such cases be the results of arbitrary, speculative desperation. This marks an important difference between, for instance, Bacon and Gerhard Richter: £42,194,500 for a Bacon is more easily justified because the work inspires this rare sense of reverence, whereas £9,000,000 for any old Richter seems like poor judgement[36]. Indeed, the Bacon here is one of those rare occasions when economic value cannot keep up with cultural value, such as when a work

---

[36] See Chapter 7, For Richter or Poorer, for a more detailed assessment of the relationship between Richter's aesthetic affect and his prices.

is so highly revered that no price could be too high. There is an element of conceit here, since whether a Bacon is worth that much due to its greatness is matter of personal taste, but when so many people – learned scholars, art dealers, artists, historians and casual viewers – seem to agree on a judgement of greatness, it is prudent to tone down the appeal to radical subjectivity and accept the majority verdict. When thinking about value, then, we would do well to remember that collective aesthetic experience will ultimately have the final word on the right price for a pickled shark and a Bacon painting alike. Greatness, after all, is in the eye of the beholder, and if enough beholders see greatness then the market has no rational choice but to follow suit.

Show and Sell

Museums occupy a curious position in the drama of the art market because while they feed it by paying £45,000,000 for a Titian, they regard themselves as outside of the capitalist game of buying and selling art. Museums sit within the public sector, while auction houses and commercial galleries are private sector entities. The links between the public and private sectors are just about as convoluted as everything else in the artworld, but the distinction can be roughly summed up as follows: public museums seek a critical distance from economic concerns of the private sector because they are custodians of art collections that are kept for the nation, while they also promote scholarship and education; private galleries and auction houses, however, are primarily focused on buying and selling for profit, helping clients to build their collections and underwriting the production of artists' work.

In both cases, there is a concern to display and disseminate art, but the ultimate goals are wildly divergent. The interesting thing is in their largely unspoken mutual dependence: the public sector buys work from the private sector, and the private sector, via liaison with artists and collectors, manages loans of artworks to exhibitions in the public sector. The connections, however, run deeper and darker than this.

One aspect of the relationship between the private and the public is the seemingly noble practice of collectors lending works to museums for blockbuster exhibitions. This is a good thing, since it enables museums to stage complete, coherent shows, and it also reflects well on the collector and their collection. But there is a trend for these acts of cultural charity to morph into instances of free advertising in such a way that the majesty of the big exhibition is used to help bump up the price of the work at auction as soon as it is off the museum wall.

Selling works, having used a major museum exhibition as free advertising, is frowned upon by public institutions because they do not want to be seen as complicit in the market. Public institutions must maintain a distance from the market, since their role is as conservators, educators and custodians – the museum is about noble stasis and perpetuity, not the wild flux and contingency of the market. The relationship between the private and public sectors is inherently unfair, since the museum needs the private collector to fill the gaps in its exhibitions. The museum ends up feeling exploited for monetary gain and dragged into a world of private finance that it has actively chosen to eschew.

The museum is bound by its covenant to make public exhibitions of exceptional quality, which often entails borrowing works from private collections; if it cannot secure the works from external sources – owing to the fact that so many important artworks reside in private collections – it fails to act within its remit. It is worth noting, however, that the collector, if they take their responsibility seriously, also acts as custodian and as such is duty bound to put the work in the public realm at every opportunity. After all, their time with the work, which may have cost them millions, is only finite and after they are gone the work will move on to someone else, but during that short time they are duty-bound to do the right thing.

The public and the private sectors need each other and the artworld needs them to co-operate if it is to achieve the dual, and sometimes fraught, goals of both showing art to the public and disseminating it to private individuals. It is indicative of the market's omnipotence that the selling of works which have been shown in museums is not enough to damage the relationship irreparably. It might ruffle feathers, but mutual dependence is a very powerful peacemaker. The public and the private operate on a network of carefully managed relationships which, on both sides, are directed towards the good of art: dissemination of art so that it can be enjoyed, studied and owned, which are all core realities of the fate of art in our societies.

We have been discussing cultural value and its connection to economic value precisely because while economics is a reality for the minority of buyers and sellers, culture is the reality for all of us, no matter where we sit in society. The strange thing is that if an artefact has a cultural value – if, that is, it is valued as an artwork with some, however great or small, significance to culture – then, insofar as it could possibly be offered for sale on the open market, it has an economic value of necessity, but the converse does not apply. The rule of thumb is that an economic value does not guarantee a cultural value because price, in the final analysis, is just a number that can be arbitrarily stipulated without reason and as such it implies nothing other than that it is subject to an exchange mechanism within an established system. Even if the price only reflects the cost of materials and labour, which may not be arbitrary, this does not thereby equate to cultural value, since that is constituted by either the aesthetic or conceptual content of the work, which determines the viewer's perception of importance, worth or greatness. In this sense, cultural and economic value are quite separate things, performing distinct functions and deriving from distinct sources. Nonetheless, in all the cases we have looked at so far there has been a clear relationship between economic and cultural value, even if we have sometimes had to untangle it in order to grasp its full consequences. As we move forwards in our investigations, the relationship will often be seen to be less clear-cut, more arbitrary and sometimes quite flagrantly absurd.

III. The Power of Myth

How narratives add value to almost anything

The value of an artwork, or an artist's body of work, can be constituted by something external to it. Art is always laden with, and sometimes burdened by, a story, a narrative which forms the basis of its value: Tracey Emin has the narrative of mad Tracey from Margate, Julien Schnabel's story is one of the meteoric rise of a swashbuckling painter with a devil-may-care attitude and van Gogh is the quintessential troubled artist struggling to paint despite his demons. These are the myths that pique interest and contextualise the art; sometimes they are created by artists and propagated by the artworld, and sometimes they are entirely fabricated by anyone other than the artist. In every case, however, myths end up as essential elements of the sales pitch, for a strong story about the genesis of art and its whole reason for being can create value – both economic and cultural – sometimes with scant regard for the qualities of the artwork itself.

These highly efficacious stories are myths in the sense that they are not written, as truth or historical fact; they are passed through generations as if they are indubitable, but they are entirely constructed, fabricated to explain reality without much, if any, concern for truth. The hallmark of myth is that it is believable, but wholly unverifiable, and yet extraordinarily powerful in explaining a history and maintaining a favourable status quo.

Here we shall consider a range of cases where value is primarily a result of myth-making; sometimes the myths will supplement a fine body of work, and sometimes they will compensate for something lacking, but they will always be the locus of cultural value. Importantly, however, whilst cultural value follows from and sometimes depends upon myth, economic value only follows contingently because the power of the myth enables it to. That is, myths do not automatically or *a priori* generate economic value, since some myths are unbelievable, faulty, boring or idiotic, in which case they generate nothing but nonsense, and certainly little in the way of economic value.

They Studied Sculpture at St Martins College…

The story of Gilbert & George is so often told and is so integral to their art that it has the authority of theological orthodoxy, but the glue that holds it all together is a pervasive myth. Two people, one artist, making Art for All in their tweed suits, dining every day in the same restaurant because they do not have a kitchen, with no friends and traditional values, all lived out to a clockwork schedule of no-frills luxury. They are incisive sculptors of modern life who live in public view, yet remain a tantalising mystery.

It is not an accident that little is said about their early lives. Gilbert Proesch was born in the Dolomites, Italy, in 1943 and George Passmore in Plymouth, Devon, in 1942. Gilbert's family were the village shoemakers and he showed an early aptitude for art with woodcarving before studying in Austria and Germany. George grew up in Totnes with a single mother and worked as a babysitter and in Selfridge's before turning to art. More detail than that would soil the immaculate conception of Gilbert & George, the Sculptors[37].

They met on the sculpture course at one of London's most renowned art colleges, St Martin's, in 1967. It was love at first sight, they say, since George was the only one who could understand Gilbert's English. St Martin's, they always say, was a grim place that rejected colour, emotions and figuration. They wanted to make art that spoke, free of jargon and fashion, to the restless heart of humanity. And so they constructed a world that has Liverpool Street station as the centre of the universe. The East End of London, they always say, is 'the most planet earth place', where an alien could land to find all human life within a hundred metre radius. Their art, against prevailing trends, paints a portrait of the turbulent ordinariness of humanity and crafts the most devotional love letter to London. Having lived for fifty years in the same Huguenot house on Fournier Street, they are practically a mobile tourist attraction, and almost all their art has been made from images of their neighbourhood[38].

They arrived in Spitalfields, penniless and passionate, at a time when the East End was truly spit and grit. The idea of living sculptures emerged from the realisation that the human being is the most artful, complex and beautiful thing. They

---

[37] More detail, although nothing earth-shattering and certainly nothing that will change the public perception, is available in Daniel Farson, *Gilbert & George: A Portrait* (London: HarperCollins, 2000).

[38] An exception being the 'Gingko Pictures' (2005), which feature leaves collected in New Yok.

found fame with *The Singing Sculpture* (1969), which involved the pair singing along to Flanagan and Allen's music hall classic 'Underneath the Arches' for eight hours a day the Sonnabend Gallery, New York. Then there were the videos, *Gordon's Makes Us Drunk* (1972) and *Bend It* (1982), featuring these two curious men in suits drinking gin or dancing erratically. And so the Sculptors became the sculpture. Using the body as a sculptural object in the format of video was an innovation in British art, echoing Bruce Nauman's similar efforts in America in the late 1960s, but for Gilbert & George it was the totality of their practice.

In order that they could make art and always be art, every detail of their daily lives was scripted and mechanised, removing all caprice and distraction – friends and kitchens, for example, were shunned because they stood in the way of the serious business of making art. Even the iconic suits were chosen as much for economy as style – the regularity and reliability, not to mention the versatility, of a two-piece suite removed the everyday chore of choosing outfits.

The pictures for which Gilbert & George are best known were born in the early 1970s. They used to make enormous, elegant, evocative charcoal drawings of themselves strolling around Hampstead Heath. When their Berlin gallerist, Konrad Fischer, asked how much he should sell them for, they said £1000 as if nobody would pay that, but a few days later the pictures sold and they had enough money to misbehave for a year, they say. And misbehave they did. They took blurry black and white photographs of themselves drinking in the pubs of Bethnal Green, which were then framed and arranged in irregular configurations and called Drinking Sculptures. The configurations echo the sensation of drunkenness, with their skewed compositions and blurry images, as if trying to visualise the haphazard, fragmented memories of the night before. These Drinking Sculptures were the start of the Gilbert & George picture, depicting the artists and their vision of a turbulent world that consists of nothing more than sex, money, race and religion.

Gilbert & George's stroke of genius was that, around about 1975, they stopped making all the work that had brought them fame. Recent history instantly became the stuff of antiquity, discontinued relics that could only be acquired at a premium, such as those early charcoal drawings which can go for anywhere up to £1,000,000. In 2008, Christie's sold *To Her Majesty* (1973), a Drinking Sculpture, for £2,2,000,000, making them one of Britain's most expensive living artists. They thus cemented their artistic reputation by creating a welter of value – for cultural value was assured by scarcity and economic value therefore followed – which would eternally justify anything else they might do. From that moment on, they set about making pictures, establishing their trademark grid and helping in no small measure to establish photography as a respectable artistic medium.

As students, Gilbert & George were appalled by St Martin's acceptance of the artworld's institutional rejection of colour and emotion, so they decided to inject both into their art. They were also sceptical about the orthodox view of sculpture as an object on a plinth, so they made themselves living sculptures. In their pictures, they depicted the degenerate and down-trodden of Spitalfields, which in the 60s and 70s was a far cry from its contemporary affluence. They made a counterpoint to their image as gentlemen in suits by producing the pictures of shit, piss, spit and spunk: piss flowers, piss streams, eight shits, shits and bums, naked shitty world, spunk on sweat, spunk on piss, and spunk money. But, again, the more they provoked the well-to-do establishment, the more entrenched in it they became – they could do no wrong. These two well-to-do gentlemen used to court considerable controversy, which is now so ubiquitous that the very idea of controversy is laughable: once you have made former director of the Tate, Sir Nicholas Serota say 'spunk' in public, there is nowhere else to go.

The indivisible remainder of their rebellion is the fact that, against all politically correct strictures, there are hardly any women in a lifetime of pictures populated by archetypal East End boys, with the exception of Queen Elizabeth II, who appears in one of the 'Scapegoating Pictures' (2014). The early grid-style pictures of the 1970s, such as 'Bad Thoughts' (1975), feature Gilbert & George looking forlorn and moody, posing in the stark rooms of their Fournier Street house prior to its renovation. In 1977, the 'Dirty Words Pictures' take the streets of London and the varied men who roam them as their subjects. During the 1980s, the pictures unashamedly focused on boys, such as the young poet David Robilliard, affectionately photographed in their Fournier Street studio, beautiful and strong, sadly immortalised after his death from an AIDS-related illness. As well as modelling for Gilbert & George, Robilliard was charged with the task of finding models for them, to which end he walked the streets of Soho and the East End looking in search of boys whom he regarded as especially photogenic. In those days, Gilbert & George paid models, one of whom was the at the time unknown actor Martin Clunes, the princely sum of £50. In 1980, they made one of their most famous pictures, *Patriots*, which shows a carefully selected lineup of East End boys – skinhead, Bangladeshi, smart, scruffy, smooth, rough, listless – stood against a wall as a representation of life in multicultural Britain.

It is difficult to see now why it was controversial, but at the time people found this selection of models, tantalising and perfect as they were, grouped under the title "Patriots" difficult to swallow. People, it seems, have always been a bit mad. Later, Gilbert & George stopped using models because the logistics were tiresome and subtracted time from the business of making Art for All. Instead, they preferred to use themselves or glimpses of strangers caught on the street; but nonetheless, the pictures always and only featured boys. Indeed, from East End tearaways to Bangladeshis to fledgling models, artists and poets, Gilbert & George's boys are simultaneously provocative and imbued with intense affection; there is both a tenderness in the pictures and a remarkable continuity in their proliferation. The Gilbert & George boys' club, whatever the 21st Century might want to say about it, remains a quaint, archaic curiosity.

However, Gilbert & George have always challenged the orthodoxy, showing in their pictures things that would offend polite society. 'The Banners' (2015) extended this to a series of commands that they, in good faith, think would improve society if adhered to. They are moral exhortations that go against the grain, or at least express what we are all thinking but dare not say publicly. There has always been that strong moral sense in Gilbert & George which simultaneously fights bigotry and, as Michael Bracewell has noted, offers an alternative in the form of equally dogmatic commands to challenge the established order[39].

These commanding works have their origins in two sources: first, in the 'Scapegoating Pictures' displayed at White Cube, London and Thaddeus Ropac, Paris, in 2014, where

---

[39] Michael Bracewell, 'Introduction', in *Gilbert & George: The Banners*, exhibition catalogue (London: White Cube, 2015)

there was a triptych which featured slogans such as "Padre is a poof" and "Cuddle a cadet"; second, the 'Dirty Words Pictures' of 1977, which showed graffiti on the streets of recession-stricken London. In all their previous work, and later in 'The Banners', Gilbert & George overstep the mark of politeness because art, if it is to speak directly to the people, cannot afford the mores of polite society or the complications of art-speak. This is the simple and sometimes brutal honesty of Gilbert & George at its most direct, the purest expression of their rejection of the established order and the purest affirmation of 'Art for All'.

Here, though, is one of the great paradoxes of Gilbert & George: while they claim to be passionate monarchists and Tories, they also espouse an uncompromising liberalism, as if they are the uneasy children of John Stuart Mill and Margaret Thatcher. A picture of David Cameron hangs on the wall of their studio at Fournier Street as they tell you they refuse to sign a petition to ban drinking on the streets of Brick Lane because they'd never do anything to stop young people having fun, even if some people call it 'anti-social behaviour'. And there is no sense at all – not a smirk nor a careless whisper – that they are peddling a contradictory blend of Conservatism and Liberalism for effect. It seems, as everything in the world of Gilbert & George does, flawlessly genuine. The craftsmanship of these little inflections and nuances of character is refined, engineered for durability and efficiency. Perhaps the politics was an affectation they concocted as part of the act in the 1960s, but now it is so well-crafted and well-honed that it seems utterly sincere, logical and necessary, as if, given time, they came to believe whatever it was they had to say to get the act going.

It is not just the politics that seems acutely contrived. The remarkable thing is that Gilbert & George's entire body of work is predicated upon a myth – namely that they are living sculptures *all the time*. The idea of these impeccably dressed, friendless, kitchenless, monarchists who live and breathe their art to a clockwork schedule – which is all part of the theatrics of being living sculptures – is essential to the creation, understanding and appreciation of their art, and yet it cannot be indubitably verified as the complete truth. The unbearable lightness of being Gilbert & George is so complete that it is impossible to know what is behind it, as if the real life of Gilbert Proesch and George Passmore is a Kantian noumena veiled by the phenomena of living sculptures. At the end of the day, when their assistant YuYi Gang has gone home and dinner is done at Mangal 2, do Gilbert and George go home, take off the suits and slump in an armchair to watch *EastEnders*? Does the act ever finish? Even their official biographer and long-time friend, Daniel Farson, concluded that what goes on behind closed doors at 12 Fournier Street is very much a mystery[40].

The myth of the living sculptures is so complete, flawless, absolute, all-encompassing that nobody has ever seen anything other than Gilbert & George the living sculptures. There is not a crack to be found anywhere in the immaculate presence of these two men whose myth proceeds them everywhere. But it is precisely this perfection that sows the seeds of doubt – how could two people so perfectly construct and sustain such a façade? The obvious answer is that it is not a façade, even if there is an element of performance to being Gilbert & George, which must have been consciously constructed at some point in the late 1960s. It seems as if there must be something

---

[40] See Daniel Farson, *Gilbert & George*, p. 29-33.

behind the appearance of these two men in their co-ordinated suits and the daily performance of their lives lived out in public. But there is nothing; nothing, at least, that anyone has ever found, for it, whatever it is, is hermetically sealed in a time capsule somewhere in 1967. The true Gilbert & George is just and only what we see, and that is all that matters.

For Gilbert & George, the art *is* the performance of the myth and the pictures are secondary to that. It is their crowning achievement that they convinced the entire artworld to play along, tight-lipped and ecstatic, always hungry for more, for it is this myth that is the conceptual ground of their work; and it is on the basis of the myth that the entire value of their work rests. A Gilbert & George picture is not just a picture to look at, it is the product of and is entirely entrenched in the myth of the living sculptures, without which the pictures simply do not make sense.

The 'Naked Shit Pictures' (1994), for instance, would be vulgar if they were not the sublime expression of Art for All and all the mythology attached to it. The myth dresses the reality of commercial success and artistic achievement in a veil of romanticism that preserves the authenticity of Art for All even with the trappings of wealth and fame. Gilbert & George closed the gap between the artist and the artwork one day in 1967 because in that gap there is only ever the inauthentic struggle of the attempt to make art with life constantly getting in the way.

But all of this is to miss the point – Gilbert & George are human beings; they are sensitive, infinitely generous, caring, loving beings who are nothing if not utterly, flawlessly sincere. So what does it matter if there is any more or less to them than living sculptures? The truth is that it does not matter what, if anything, is behind the myth or whether they ever take a break from being Gilbert & George because they are one of the greatest artworks to have ever been conceived. The myth gives depth and meaning to the pictures, for the 'Naked Shit Pictures', by two perfect gentlemen, are the pinnacle of cosmopolitan social commentary. As such, all Gilbert & George's value is cultural, since it is the myth, the very Being of Gilbert & George, that makes the work significant, interesting and of continued relevance to art; the economic value of a given artwork is just a necessary evil of working within the confines of the commercial artworld and of living an expensive lifestyle in a capitalist society.

It is as if Gilbert & George set out to find the truth of human life and discovered that only the objectivity of a living sculpture could grasp the ineffable spirit of human striving. None of this is to say that there is nothing interesting in the pictures, but only that the myth of Gilbert & George is precisely what makes them valuable. The value industry is delighted with Gilbert & George because it need not concern itself with scholarship or analysis of pictures to create value for this exemplary artist duo, for the myth has always already done the hard graft. All a sales person has to do is to explain to a client how Gilbert & George live and value is added and the work is sold without any reference to the art at all. They will take their myth and ultimately their art to the grave, leaving us with only the pictures, as if to say, 'all my life I give you nothing, and still you ask for more'[41].

---

[41] This is the title of a pair of self-portraits by Gilbert & George from 1970.

The Great Dictator, or Rebel with a Cause

It is not only artists who use myths to create value for themselves. A collector can forge their own myth to add value to their collection and to build the reputations of the artists they collect. In such a case, the collector is using a self-styled myth to make themselves desirable as someone whom artists and the market alike will want to do business with. After all, a little mystique goes a long way in business if you know how to handle it, and nobody knew that better than a certain collector whose myth preceded him everywhere and who once ruled the artworld.

This collector, a millionaire who lives on a diet of boiled eggs and iced coffee, is steeped in a myth of his own making. He is an altruist and a patron; he is a tyrant and a menace. He made the careers of the day's top artists, scandalised the artworld with his unconventional dealings and then wrote a book about how to be the worst you can be. Imagine that this enigma, so prominent in the lives of so many, nonetheless remained a reclusive mystery who could always be identified by his trademark blue suit, buttoned-up white shirt and shock of black hair. There you have Charles Saatchi, the artworld's Wizard of Oz. But who is Charles Saatchi? And is he friend or foe of the artworld? One thing is certain, his self-styled myth as the mover and shaker of cool young art added value to every work he touched and every artist he dealt with.

The British artworld of today has three people at its foundation, who, in their own ways, created the scene. Damien Hirst was the artist who typified a movement, earning fame and fortune with works that people thought were new and shocking. Jay Jopling was the young, erudite, charming art dealer who choreographed the shenanigans in both the market and the media, and established White Cube, one of the world's exceptional contemporary art galleries. And then there was Saatchi: the aloof millionaire who would buy up an entire show of some young unknown artist, sending the market loopy, and then show them in his plush Hampstead gallery to great ecstasy. If Jopling was the mover trying to build a career as a gallerist, Saatchi was the shaker whose only vested interest was his own money. This made Saatchi powerful, sought-after and ever so slightly dangerous because as a man seemingly driven by whimsey he could sell just as capriciously as he could buy. And that he did. This is the crux of Saatchi's unique position and the source of his controversy[42].

Saatchi's mythology as the heroic mystery-man of art collecting was designed to make him seem, in the eyes of artists, a desirable, delectable patron; it was a smokescreen to cover the reality of his shortcomings. Stallabrass sums up the Saatchi enigma perfectly by saying his reputation was that he was known for 'buying very cheap, and in bulk, and selling dear'[43]. He was an adman from the ruthless world of business who knew what he wanted and could manipulate the system to get it on his own terms. To counter this, Saatchi made himself mysterious by behaving as if his buying-power was an act of conjuring. He quickly gained almost messianic status among young artists, who felt that the laying of his hands on their work would assure their careers for life. And it did. For a time in the 1990s, everything Saatchi touched turned to gold; emerging artists were desperate for him to turn up at their shows, unannounced and before the private view began, to wave his magic wand. The artworld had never known a force

---

[42] A brilliant and unflinching account of Saatchi's foibles, professional and personal, is revealed by Alison Fendley, *Commercial Break: The Inside Story of Saatchi & Saatchi*, (London: Hamish Hamilton, 1995).
[43] Stallabrass, *High Art Lite*, 227.

like Saatchi, with his buying-power and his exquisite taste, his eye for the next big thing. The man was a living myth.

The real mystique of Saatchi lies in the fact that his unconventional methods were very good for art, but not so good for the market. Saatchi's cavalier attitude towards the market emerged early on. During the 1980s, at his advertising firm, Saatchi & Saatchi, he invested a very great deal in a respectable and, at the time, fashionable, art collection. He had extensive holdings of the great blue-chip artists of the day, including Schnabel, Koons and Kiefer. Saatchi's voracious collecting aided and abetted the great art boom of the 80s and played no small part in the meteoric rise of these artists, who at the time were not yet household names, even if they were fairly well established by the time Saatchi got to them. As we know, the market migrates where the money is and it is money which makes artists' careers, so Saatchi was in his element – the illusion of power over, not just art, but over the lives of human beings, bought with a simple transaction.

At the end of the 1980s, after a decade of boom, Saatchi made a dramatic decision, which contravened every rule of the art market. He decided to sell practically his entire collection. This is detrimental to the market, since selling all your Schnabels at once makes Schnabels less rare and less precious, since suddenly there are so many available, causing prices to plummet. Saatchi has gleefully done this repeatedly throughout his art-collecting career. Not only does this break the rules of the art market, but it also contravenes the standard operating procedure of capitalism itself, which depends on a fine and endless balance between scarcity and abundance. This behaviour earned Saatchi the wrong sort of legendary status in market circles.

Saatchi became another sort of legend in exhibition circles by being both the man about town and the man who is nowhere to be seen. It is well-attested how Saatchi would silently turn up to an exhibition unannounced, skulk around unseen and go home having bought up the entire show. Artists loved this, not just because their unknown, unrecognized work was bought by an important collector, but also because the sheer ghostly mystique of it all was riveting. It seemed like a good thing that a powerful collector remained so aloof, since although he was supporting the arts, he was not taking the limelight from the artists.

After the 'Sensation' exhibition of his YBA collection at the Royal Academy of Art, London, in 1997, and as those artists became more independent of his patronage, Saatchi's powers began to wane. But that was less to do with his collecting than with his obstinate behaviour. Popular rumour has it that the Tate had to cancel a Hirst retrospective in the early 2000s because Saatchi would not lend key Hirst pieces; he also irked the Hayward Gallery in 2011, refusing to lend Emin's *My Bed* for a retrospective. He ignited a spat with Hirst over the display of a Mini Cooper decorated with Hirst's trademark spots: Saatchi proudly showed it in his gallery, much to Hirst's disdain, who said it did not count as one of his artworks. Eventually Hirst bought back from Saatchi many of his own works. In the Principality of Art, you do not mess with Prince Damien, even if you are one of the men who led him to the throne.

Throughout the first decade of the 21st Century, Saatchi increasingly found himself out in the cold. He met a frosty reception when he tried to invent a new movement in painting, which he called New Neurotic Realism, celebrating the great Dexter Dalwood as its chief proponent. He tried, with a series of lacklustre shows of his latest acquisitions, to rekindle the fire of the 90s, but nothing ever caught on again. And there was no problem with the art, since Saatchi – as ever – was collecting the hottest tickets, such as Dalwood, who was nominated for the Turner Prize in 2010 and remains one of the great painters of the century. Moreover, Saatchi continued to demonstrate a keen eye for the latest emerging talent, collecting the likes of Murillo, Christian Rosa and Ibrahim Mahama. The problem was Saatchi himself, who had fallen out of favour and was desperately trying to make amends by staging exhibitions that claimed to have identified new movements and trends just like in the good old days. Except the good old says were gone, seemingly for ever.

Saatchi's mistake was that he played the game his own way; he thought his money – and the good it transparently did for art – entitled him to make his own rules and assumed that the alluring persona of the aloof uber-collector would forgive all. Both art and the market are rule-governed, conventional systems that operate within defined parameters, so there are rules and systems which govern the way things are done. Furthermore, art and the market depend upon everyone, without exception, playing by the rules; even the artists and gallerists who occasionally make waves by 'doing things differently' are playing by the rules. The market, if it is to function at all, demands that everyone act within decent expectation all the time. So when Saatchi sells almost his entire collection of Kiefers, flooding the market and messing with the prices, he is not playing by the rules, and it was the cumulative effect of years of this behaviour that was his downfall.

Saatchi the rule-breaker, the benefactor, the man of exceptional taste, the recluse and the man-about-town is a myth of his own making. The production of this myth was a calculated effort to ensure that his notoriety preceded him so that artists would be seduced into selling cheap and the market would accept his transgressions.

The value of Saatchi's collection is partly a function of the works within it, but it is also a function of his myth. The logic goes like this: if an artist X is collected by Saatchi, who has great taste and spending power, then work by X must be of extremely high quality. In other words, Saatchi had built himself up to the point where a work good enough for Saatchi is desirable to everyone. Saatchi's myth is the myth of the supreme taste-maker.

Not being one to hold on to works for too long (another *faux pas* in the market), Saatchi quickly and regularly cashed in on this mythological acumen, turning a healthy profit every time. For example, Saatchi bought Marcus Harvey's *Myra* (1995) for £11,000, basked in the controversy it caused and later sold it for £100,000. The inflation of the price was doubtless spearheaded by the vast amount of press attention it received, but underlying that was the fact that, despite the condemnation, Saatchi had discovered an important work of art and brought it to the world. This fed the myth and created value in two ways: first, it demonstrated that Saatchi had an eye that could see things which everyone else was blind to; and second, as with all the other artists he collected in the 1990s, it assured the world that Harvey was somebody worth taking note of and bumped up his prices accordingly.

Saatchi illustrates a critical lesson: in the fundamentally undemocratic artworld, anyone can be a dictator, but only the ones who choose to use that power to simultaneously help the goodies (the art) and fight the baddies (the market) will prevail. Saatchi is good for art because he entered a closed system and rejected its rules, and there is nothing more refreshing and vital than a conscientious rule-breaker who uses his own myth to create value for himself and others.

Although Saatchi created economic value in quite obvious ways, the cultural value he generated is longer-lasting and more relevant to anyone who is not Saatchi. He was, after all, one of the three people who spearheaded the YBA movement, and so his self-styled mythology enabled him to exert great influence by buying and selling whatever his heart desired, where it just so happened that whatever his heart desired, for a time at least, was always the next big thing in art.

How did his myth help him to do this? Simply put, it made him an attractive proposition – of all the collectors out there, Saatchi seemed powerful, mysterious, capricious, endowed with good taste and uncommonly uninterested in the limelight. It was an irresistible combination that generated value for everyone whom he came into contact with, but the myth of the magical value-generator turned out to be exactly that – a myth that could not, in the end, survive everybody's exasperation with Saatchi's dealings. For Saatchi, once the love was lost, so was his ability create value of any significant kind.

A Rolling Schnabel Gathers No Sparks

The career of the American painter Julian Schnabel demonstrates how the critical credibility of an artist's work can depend almost entirely on their self-made myth and, conversely, that once the myth is gone, there is little left to be said about the art.

Culture has a selective memory because it diminishes the thrill of the Now to admit that we have seen it all before, so when a new celebrity artist turns up the old ones must be usurped. This is what happened to Schnabel, whose myth was simply that he was the greatest artist alive, the 'closest thing to Picasso', he said, and, for some time, everyone believed it. Nietzsche perhaps had Schnabel in mind when he said, 'a poet could say that God has placed forgetfulness as a doorkeeper at the threshold of the temple of human dignity'[44]. As Schnabel opened his first exhibition in London for 15 years, it was time to wonder why we forgot and to remind ourselves that the myth of this mammoth of an artist was once a very powerful thing, even if, on his return to the artworld, there was hardly a trace of it left[45]. Here we have an example of an artist's self-made myth creating immense economic value, but when all the excitement dies down and the myth fizzles out, there is very little in the way of cultural value left.

In the 1980s, Schnabel was the prototype Hirst, gaining big money and celebrity status so quickly that even people who were not quite sure what he did knew an anecdote about him. In person, he is a captivating, formidable presence with a mischievous sense of humour that is underpinned by a carefully constructed aloofness. When he speaks, he stares into the horizon, as if waiting for the words to materialise on the ether, and he always says the opposite of what you think he might or should say. The man and his art possess the discrete charm of an intelligence which is veiled by a seductive bravado. Contrary to the Legend of Schnabel, which tells of wild riots and loose morals, he is both more thoughtful and less vulgar than one might think. He seems disarmingly sincere

---

[44] Friedrich Nietzsche, *Human, All-Too-Human*, Volume I, trans. R. J. Hollingdale (Cambridge and New York: Cambridge University Press, 1996), §92.
[45] 'Every Angel Has a Dark Side', Dairy Art Centre, London, 23 April – 27 July 2014.

and devoted to his art, for example, when he says that he does not represent anything in his paintings, but he only presents things. Schnabel's paintings possess the urgency of a postmodern orientation towards history that seamlessly melds with an individual style; but they are boldly executed and thereby rather slapdash, as if the man has better things to do than painting. It is that visceral self-confidence that the artworld fell in love with and made Schnabel an expensive, trailblazing celebrity artist.

The Schnabel story is full of thrills and careless whispers. Having gained his BFA from the University of Houston, an audacious Schnabel masterminded his return to his native New York via the Independent Study Programme at the Whitney with slides of his paintings encased between slices of bread. At the age of 24 he held his first solo museum show at the Contemporary Art Center, Houston, and four years later sold out the entirety of his first solo show at Mary Boone Gallery before it even opened. Having participated in the 1980 Venice Biennale, Schnabel gained joint representation by Mary Boone and Leo Castelli – of Warhol and Rauschenberg fame – with a major exhibition in 1981.

In the 1980s, Schnabel quickly ingratiated himself with the bustling New York scene, hanging out with Andy Warhol and Basquiat, walking around in his silk pyjamas, travelling the world with exhibitions, going to parties and saying outlandish things like 'I'm the closest thing to Picasso you'll see in this fucking life'. He was brash and arrogant, as were his paintings, often at billboard scale, which he mostly made from broken plates, tarpaulin and mirrors, sometimes weathered in a hurricane or dragged on the tarmac behind a speeding car. He did features for glossy lifestyle magazines, posing shirtless at his Long Island studio. By 1984 Schnabel was a gossip column regular: when he dumped his loyal gallerists for Pace, Leo Castelli wrote a scathing article in the *New York Times* comparing him to King Kong. Nowadays, it is said, nobody who worked with him in the 80s will talk about him, perhaps still wounded by the trauma or subject to a gagging order.

An artist whose commercial success seems to know no bounds and who narcissistically compares himself to Picasso is destined for a nasty fall. By the time of his 1987 mid-career retrospective at the Whitney, Schnabel's Cristal ball began to foresee hard times ahead. Although the fashion in contemporary art had changed and the market slowed in the face of recession, the Fall of Schnabel was as much about personality as it was about painting. A critical backlash concluded he epitomised the ugly excess of the decade and his work was suddenly denounced as pretentious and tacky. Legend has it that a particularly cutting review of his Whitney show said that the paintings, hardly a few years old, had not stood the test of time. Even though he remained a prolific painter with an almost religious devotion to his art, the artworld was exhausted and looking elsewhere. Schnabel retreated into film, directing the highly acclaimed *Basquiat* and *The Diving Bell and the Butterfly*, as well as launching Javier Bardem's career with *Before Night Falls*.

Following a hiatus between 2002 and 2011, however, Schnabel returned, most notably with a retrospective at the Museo Correr in Venice during the 2013 Biennale and an epic show at the Brant Foundation, Connecticut. His 2014 exhibition at the Dairy Art Centre, London, with concurrent shows at Gagosian and at Karma, New York, and Dallas Contemporary, hailed the Second Coming of Schnabel, bringing him to a new audience, a new generation of artists and a more self-consciously calculated artworld.

But the fire did not ignite as it had before. When he started out, painting was apparently dead, the market was famished and there were so many free column inches just waiting for artists to make a spectacle of themselves. Throughout the 1980s, Schnabel trailblazed his way through life claiming to be the greatest artist alive. And for a time, as we have seen, the market and the press believed it, but on his return to the fray it was difficult to see what the fuss had been about. His new paintings seemed stuck in the 1980s, they paled in comparison to the contemporary artworld of 2014. It became apparent that the Schnabel myth was tied to an earlier time and had no application in the present; a once great artist was a relic in his own times.

That is not to say that Schnabel himself felt anything different. In a promotional film for his string of 2014 exhibitions, Schnabel says, with his trademark absolute earnestness, 'It is a privilege to engage in something that is the antitheses of reason. I guess when God created the world He maybe got a little tired at the end, so He only put a certain amount of things...in the course of those seven days. And maybe poetry was something He left out, and He left that for humans to do'[46]. Those are not the words of a man who has left behind his youthful grandiose self-image.

It is difficult not to view Schnabel through the misty lens of an art market that defies economic trends and an artworld saturated with celebrity artists who peddle glittering conceptualism to hedge fund managers. In this light, the materials, methods and myths of Schnabel's paintings somehow, against all odds, seem divested of their former glory as commercial products. The new paintings are laced with

---

[46] *In the Course of Seven Days*, directed by Porfino Munoz (distributed by Nowness.com).

Schnabel's restless ambition to make painting matter, but with the passing of time and the onward march of art history, they lack the heroic quality of his own myth. Schnabel re-emerged into an artworld that had, after his nine-year break, all but forgotten him; without the sensuous immediacy of the myth, the paintings appeared flat and slightly confounding, laced with delusions of grandeur, such as when he painted himself as Velázquez.

There was a time when such an egotistical gesture would have made sense because the man who thought he was the contemporary Picasso had painted it; but it was painted by a man who used to be the man who thought he was the contemporary Picasso, which does not have the same ring to it. The myth of the greatest living painter, the closest thing to Picasso, was something Schnabel created and perpetuated in an extraordinarily resourceful and self-conscious way through the magazine features, photo shoots, bitching in gossip columns, wearing silk pyjamas to nightclubs and oversized paintings made by unconventional methods. But when all that performance ground to a halt, so did the glory and the faith in the glory.

All of this certainly created economic value because it defined Schnabel and his art as a distinct, marketable commodity, for to buy a Schnabel painting was to buy a lifestyle, as well as a product and a mythology. However, the myth also gave the paintings themselves a kind of shimmering grandeur, creating the impression that they were great, historically significant paintings. For a time in the 1980s, everyone bought into this notion of Schnabel's cultural value, since a vast painting adorned with broken plates and depicting an inchoate scene of minimal interest must be a great painting and an innovation if it is created by the closest thing to

Picasso. It must be, they assured themselves. But as the years wore on and the myth wore out into the 21st Century, it became apparent that they were not great paintings and Schnabel was not a great painter – that was all an illusion, sustained by market success. That is not to say Schnabel is a bad painter, he has his moments of insight and sometimes captures the sheen of emotion in the surface of the pigment, but, especially in the glory days, aesthetically, he is little more than a Poundland Kiefer.

The myth of Schnabel, the closest thing to Picasso, constitutes the cultural value of the paintings, and once that myth is buried in the annals of history, the paintings fail to resonate. Nonetheless, Schnabel somehow still smoulders with a constant, iridescent light that flickers in and out of consciousness but never entirely burns out. Schnabel became a cipher of himself, both there and not there simultaneously. It is as if he is the exception that proves the rule, as ee cummings said, 'a rolling Schnabel gathers no sparks/the same hold true for Karl the Marks'[47].

The Starry Heavens Above, the Moral Law Within

Anselm Kiefer uses myth as the content of his art, unlike Schnabel, who uses it as the content of his very being. Kiefer dreams of turning Switzerland into a maritime nation: if only, he thinks, we could discover the mythical universal solvent – the *Alkahest* – that has preoccupied alchemists for centuries, all the land could be dissolved until Switzerland opens out on to the sea. It sounds like the rambling of a madman, but it is the

---

[47] Adapted from ee cummings, 'Ballad of an Intellectual', in *AnOther* (New York: Liveright, 2000).

perfect distillation of an artist whose entire practice is an interweaving of myth with history and alchemy with art. Indeed, Kiefer's appropriation of mythology, especially of the philosopher's stone, bears a remarkable analogy with the workings of the art market that so gleefully supports him. For Kiefer, myth is the subject of his art and art is only a myth that sustains our faith in a humanity that scarcely deserves it.

Kiefer was born in 1945, so unlike his older contemporaries – Baselitz, for instance, who endured the firebombing of Dresden – he never witnessed the Second World War first-hand. This one biographical fact alone accounts for an entire career: Kiefer was thrown into a world of profound mourning, ravaged by a monumental event that changed the course of history, with the wounds weeping and the weight of the narrative of conflict on his shoulders. Having been thrust into the midst of it and having not witnessed a thing, all of this was, for Kiefer, a matter of the utmost urgency. It is for this very reason that the line between myth and history dissolves in art for Kiefer.

Art, he has said, is not entertainment; it is difficult. A great deal of Kiefer's work centres on Germany after the Second World War – what it is, what it is not, what it could be. When he started out, in the late 1960s, it was indeed difficult, since the history – as it always is – was just being written. This is art that is so far from entertainment that it swells into a nightmare on an industrial scale: Kiefer was confronting the reality of a past that was, at the time, hardly three decades old, but it is not at all obvious that these works can ever be innocuous.

Kiefer's preoccupation with alchemy and myth underwrite his exploration of the living themes of post-war Germany, allowing him to draw in references from philosophy, poetry, mysticism, music and religion. But this does not decorate the work, it deepens its humanity and urgency by introducing an irrepressible timelessness. It illustrates that whatever trials humanity faces now have always persisted at its core. Kiefer, although overtly historical, is always and essentially existential. Alchemy and myth, for Kiefer, represent humanity's internal conflicts between ambition and innovation or fear and ignorance, which have characterised every moment of history. But they also map on to distinct strands of the artworld that Kiefer sits, nearly indestructibly, at the top of.

The alchemist's quest for the philosopher's stone – the substance that transforms lead into gold – is a persistent theme in Kiefer's work. He explored it on a monumental scale in 'Il Mistero della Catedralli' (White Cube Bermondsey, 2011), a series of works based on Fulcanelli, an obscure figure who claimed to have transformed 100 grams of lead into gold and wrote a book claiming that the architecture of Europe's great cathedrals contain hidden signs that unlocked this secret. Kiefer recast Albert Speer's Tempelhof Airport in the role of the cathedral in a series of vast paintings that aligned the Third Reich's expansionism with the search for the philosopher's stone. Hitler's project, in this view, was like the search for the philosopher's stone – futile, sociopathic, deluded and immoral. Tempelhof, one of the first commercial airports to have ever been built, stands in for one of Fulcanelli's cathedrals, implying that the secret, not of the philosopher's stone, but of the truth of German history, is contained within the stones of Tempelhof, which stand as sickening reminders – symptoms, even – of exceptional human error. And here Kiefer and Fulcanelli necessarily diverge: Fulcanelli had to re-interpret and analyse the architecture of the cathedrals to reach the secret of the philosopher's stone, whereas Tempelhof speaks for itself –

Kiefer needs to add nothing to it in order to make it say what it does. The message, in the final analysis, is that history contains brute facts that cannot reasonably be denied, whereas myth is so much interpretation. That is not to say history is not open to interpretation, of which Kiefer is abundantly aware, but Kiefer is eccentric, not mad or morally corrupt, as perhaps Fulcanelli may have been, so he cannot but acknowledge that Tempelhof is exactly what it is, even if it can also be re-interpreted as something else.

It is often ambiguous whether Kiefer thinks alchemy is a genuine science or a symptom of lunacy, but it is difficult not to see the implication that blue chip artists are always alchemists. In his own case, Kiefer turns crumbling masses of paint, lead, resin and earth into the gold of artworld stardom, so alchemy and art are two sides of the same coin: craft, technique, ambition and luck converge to generate fortunes out of almost nothing at all, which is a fine analogy for the workings of the value industry that routinely uses myth to generate value.

History is about real-world events, whereas myth is about human narratives that have only a contingent relation to reality. Starting from the brute, sometimes uncomfortable, facts, Kiefer is interested in narratives, particularly the way history tells stories that are ultimately open-ended and subject to interpretation; he is also sympathetic to the idea that emotion is as powerful as intellect. And here is the crux of why Kiefer is interested in myth and history concurrently, and why he sometimes seems to overlay them with each other: history and myth – as they are written and told – are narratives, they are the stories we tell to explain how and why we got here. An example of how a concern for narrative can intermingle myth and history is the way that Kiefer is obsessed with the Russian

Futurist Velimir Khlebnikov, who conducted years of historical research to conclude that a major naval battle occurs every 317 years. This appeals to Kiefer because he thinks history, the moment it is written, is subject to interpretation, which further muddies the authority of the historical narrative.

In art, myth supersedes any hint of truth: the market sells stories that incidentally have paintings attached to them, for it is not unusual to hear a salesperson in a commercial gallery waxing lyrical about the work's genesis, the artist's biography, anything but the artwork itself, because stories sell. Kiefer's canvases, with fleets of lead submarines and sunflowers attached to them, are the by-product of a narrative that makes the rich feel enlightened and cultured. In buying a Kiefer, a collector is demonstrating their passion for and intellectual appreciation of history; they thus buy into the mythology without realising they are a part of it.

Legend has it that Kiefer's paintings are sold with a disclaimer to the effect that decay is built into the unwieldy masses so that collectors cannot complain when clumps fall off at even the lightest breeze. Art is only alchemy and myth, but it is also just matter that, like everything else humanity busies itself with, is subject to entropy. The message in the end seems to be that, although life, history, humanity and evil seem very important, it all just goes to dust in the end. In this way, Kiefer echoes Kant's dying thought: there is nothing greater and so true as the starry heavens above and the moral law within.

Narratives and Markets

In all the cases we have considered, myth has played a role in creating value. For Gilbert & George, a pervasive myth of living sculptures underwrites the art to the extent that it, and it alone, gives the work meaning. Saatchi created a mythological version of himself in order to be a desirable patron and to build the reputations of the artists he collected. Schnabel created the myth of himself as the greatest living artist, which created his cultural value and was accepted wholesale but never survived the passing of time, leaving his art looking rather anaemic. And Kiefer weaves myth into the subject of his art to demonstrate that history and art themselves are subject to productive, efficient mythologies.

These myths create value in the sense that they appeal to the human desire for a narrative that simultaneously makes sense of the world and challenges our pre-existing beliefs about it. Gilbert & George, for instance, make pictures that reflect the ever-changing socio-cultural landscape of London, infusing it all with a liberal-conservativism that forces us to ask questions of our beliefs and ideas about how to live in and deal with the modern world. Similarly, Saatchi takes the art market as we know it, constructs the appearance of playing the game, while consciously flouting all the rules that he is supposed to be bound by, leading to a critical evaluation of those rules and the system in which they operate. Cultural value is produced by the fact that the four myth-makers we have analysed all take an idiosyncratic stance on what art is and how it should be practiced, thereby marking themselves out as making a discrete, individual contribution to culture, without which humanity would surely be impoverished. Economic value follows because the art market, like any other, seeks distinct products to sell, whether it is a unique brand of art for all, the erudite eye of a collector, the self-proclaimed Picasso of his generation or the quintessential myth-maker.

Myth adds another string to our bow in understanding value because it highlights the way in which value – cultural or economic – need not be derived from the artwork itself. Whilst the aesthetic and conceptual concept of the work, as we saw with Hirst, may inform a judgement of value, myths that are built out of ideas external to the work can equally perform the same task because they play a necessary role in making narratives. That is not to say that, in the examples here elucidated, there is no connection between the myth on the outside and the aesthetics or concepts on the inside of the work of art, but only that it is the stuff on the outside that is doing most of the work. Consider the counterfactual scenarios: if it were not for the calculated myth-making, we would have become bored by the sameness of forty-odd years of Gilbert & George pictures, Saatchi would have been rejected by the market, Schnabel would have been seen to be a charlatan and Kiefer would be denounced a madman. But the narratives they weave ensure that the story is always fresh, always intoxicating and just on the right side of believable.

We are yet to see cases where myths fail to add any value at all, but for now, the key thing is that they create value because they are carefully constructed and ultimately believable in virtue of the fact that they constitute the meaning of the artwork and thus supply its cultural value. The art market, given that it is putting a price on the priceless and trading in the highest pursuit of the human spirit as if it is a mere commodity, is an inhuman beast. Myths humanise this process, which art cannot survive without, by creating narratives that tie up all the loose ends and bring order to the otherwise messy and delicately vulgar business of the art market by neatly suggesting an appropriate economic value for the priceless.

IV. Authenticity and History

How to derive values from facts

In philosophy and the social sciences, there is a much-discussed distinction between facts and values, for to describe a state of affairs is not necessarily to evaluate it. In moral philosophy, for example, it is said that a value cannot be derived from a fact: the fact of the matter may be that David owes money to Immanuel, but it does not follow that David ought to pay it back because statements of fact are value-free; that is, they contain no sense of what *ought* to be the case following from what *is* the case. The standard criticism of this form of the distinction is that the moral obligation to pay back money owed is contained within the social structure of lending. Plenty of philosophers thus reject the fact-value distinction with good reason. In sociology, the fact that there are families with one male parent and one female parent who are married does not entail the value that this ought to be the case everywhere. There is nothing inherent in the state of affairs which implies or necessitates any value judgement at all. Sociologists will tend, therefore, to accept that a fact does not entail a value, as it seems proper and circumspect in the aforementioned case.

In art, it seems obvious that values can be derived from facts at least some of the time. Indeed, lest pricing should be entirely arbitrary, there has to be a sense in which (monetary) values arise quite organically from facts. For example, although much in art is subjective, economic value can be elegantly derived from certain facts of history and provenance. The prices of artworks can eschew the fact-value distinction, even while we leave the philosophers and sociologists to squabble amongst themselves, because economic value often derives from claims of authenticity. Furthermore, as we saw in the case of the fake Chagall, certain facts of authenticity and history play a decisive role in determining cultural value.

It has been shown how value can derive from the aesthetic or conceptual qualities of the artwork and from the myth surrounding it, but it is much less clear how specifically economic value can ultimately inhere in an artefact. Artworks are, after all, often made of materials that themselves have little monetary value: paint, pencils, paper and canvases are inexpensive compared to the prices of drawings and paintings; even sculptures, which are made by skilled artisans and of more costly materials such as marble end up selling for considerably more than they cost to produce. Some artworks, such as those of Martin Creed, are made of extraordinarily mundane materials like blue-tack and chairs, which should not be priced at more than a few pounds. Even those artworks, such as those of Hirst, that are made of gold and industrially produced diamonds, sell for vastly more than the sum of their constituent parts. What, then, is it that causes artworks, which are mere stuff, to command such high prices?

There are a number of answers to this question, chief among them is how myth creates value, but the case of the fake Chagall painting hinted at another, more factual, answer: artefacts can be bought and sold for indefinitely high prices owing to the power of a single concept – authenticity. The idea that X is an authentic product of Y is all that is needed to generate a price for anything at all, for when one buys an artwork or a designer suit, the price is justified by its being an authentic product of that artist or designer.

An appeal to the fact of authenticity, or, as we shall see, the facts of history, demonstrates that the value industry is not always or only arbitrary: when value is created out of authenticity, which is more or less an objective science. Authenticity is so powerful a concept in art that it can sway economic value regardless of aesthetics, concepts and myths. Similarly, when construed as the recording of a series of facts about what happened and when, history can add value. Indeed, authenticity is itself an historical matter, as is provenance.

It is worth noting at the outset, however, that the price is not necessarily right only if the artwork is authentic. If authenticity were the only criteria for setting prices, then there would be no logic to setting different prices for different artists or for different works by the one artist, since there are not degrees of authenticity – a thing is either the genuine article or it is not. The fact is that one Picasso is better than another, for example, so even where authenticity is assured a difference in price is made on grounds of cultural value. An authentic work can be under- or over-priced, then, if it is accorded an inappropriate cultural value. Authenticity only has final say on economic value where it has first been disputed, but crucially in these cases it is only authenticity that can decide the economic value because a sound judgement of cultural value depends upon authenticity being assured in the first instance. In cases where there never was any question over authenticity, we should assume the price already accounts for the fact that the work is an authentic product of whatever it claims to be.

Laughing all the Way to the Banksy

Authenticity becomes an issue of grave concern as soon as street art begins to gain currency on the market. An attempt to transform a highly nuanced artform into just another commodity, to generate economic value by cashing in on the kudos of street art, is guided by the popular idea that, until it is exhibited in a certain way, street art is vandalism and a nuisance. In 2015, seven Banksy murals were removed from the streets of London by a cowboy art dealership called Stealing Banksy?[48] Not only does this teach us a lesson about the essential nature of street art, it demonstrates how the market sometimes serves as the guardian of the integrity of art.

The works were sold to private collectors in an online auction organised by Stealing Banksy?, who claim to act as independent agents – independent, that is, of auction houses, city councils, galleries and, of course, Banksy himself. The company claims it does not sanction, encourage or order the theft of Banksy works or damage to private property. Instead, it acts on the instruction of landlords, whose properties have been desecrated by Banksy, in the removal of murals through a process they call 'sensitive salvage'. Through a painstaking and expensive process, they extract the mural from the wall and reconstitute it elsewhere. They are, then, operating within the

---

[48] The name of the organisation includes the question mark, presumably as a wry, self-conscious, but entirely unamusing, joke.

great art historical tradition that gave Spain's Museo del Prado Francisco Goya's *Saturn Devouring His Son* (c. 1819-23), which was cautiously lifted from Goya's own dining room wall.

The practise of surgically removing paintings from walls is a long and noble tradition of rescuing important artworks from decay and destruction, so on the surface it looks as if Stealing Banksy? is acting within the bounds of decency, but there is an essential difference[49]. In the case of Goya, the paintings were removed in 1874, long after Goya had fled to France in 1823 and after the house had changed hands several times. The removal was ordered by the then occupant of the house, Emile d'Erlanger, for fear that the work was severely deteriorating. The process was conducted by experts from the Prado, who transferred the painting to canvas and painstakingly restored it. Not only would one reasonably think this met with Goya's approval, since it was done in the name of preservation, the works were subsequently donated to a national collection.

The Banksy case, however, has very different motives, even if it appears to be working within the same tradition. Stealing Banksy? considers that it is creating value by means of preservation and dissemination. Superficially, Stealing Banksy? might appear to be committing an act of cultural altruism: it looks as if it is disseminating Banksy's work through the channels of the market, giving it that peculiar kudos of a cultural product which not only has value in itself, but also has the democratic mobility which enables art to be seen the world over.

This appearance is a mere conceit which hides the fact that the company exists purely for the promotion of private

---

[49] Records indicate that the technique dates back at least to 59 BC, where Vitruvius reports that paintings were cut out of the walls in Sparta and transported to the Continuum.

interests, which does moral violence to public art. Stealing Banksy? acts in the interests of landlords who claim they never asked for their walls to become artworks, who suffer from the continued attention the works draw and who face potential losses to their businesses if their buildings are given grade II listing status because of the murals. The landlords' litany of complaints is heart-breaking, for nobody should be coerced into receiving custodianship of a great work of art. Indeed, Stealing Banksy? says that it does not make any money from serving the landlords interests in this way. Since even the most culturally sensitive dealership still wants to turn a profit, the only explanation is that Stealing Banksy? genuinely thinks it is performing a public service.

Art galleries, auction houses and the whole infrastructure of the artworld exist to build confidence and preserve integrity. To exhibit in a gallery is to be recognised by the gallerist, to sell in an auction house is to have provenance confirmed, to be reviewed in a respected publication is to gain critical esteem – these processes exist in order to confer legitimacy upon art. But Stealing Banksy? sold the works to private collectors in a manner which is nothing short of clandestine: the seven murals were displayed in an entry-fee charging exhibition, staged in the conference suite of a hotel, before being sold through an online auction. Anybody can hire a space and stage an exhibition, sell art on their website and get reviewed on somebody's blog, which is no bad thing, but that does nothing to demonstrate anything about the quality or authenticity of the work. Those Banksy murals were led to an uncertain and squalid fate in being denied passage through the proper channels.

This is a bitter pill to swallow in the age of do-it-yourself success and social media marketing, but in art you need the right people behind you to gain credibility. You do not have to have Jay Jopling fighting your corner, but you do have to have a gallerist who is willing – and this is the crucial thing – to put their reputation on the line by showing your work in their gallery. It is that risk that sounds a chime of confidence in the quality and integrity of your art. It is for this reason that gallerists, critics and curators are inundated with a constant stream of artists begging for their support. Stealing Banksy? opted to forgo the standard route to legitimacy in favour of a quick and easy sale, very much to the detriment of art.

There are two serious issues here. Firstly, there is the issue of who owns the Banksy works and who therefore has the right to remove and sell them. It is too simplistic to say that the landlords are the rightful owners, for while they may well own the buildings, it does not follow that they own the artworks. A legal definition of the situation is as follows: the canvas on which the artwork is painted, the building, is owned by the landlord, but the artwork consists in the image, which is the intellectual property of the artist. There are two separate entities here with two different owners. Therefore, the landlord must prove that they can legally take the intellectual property along with the wall. There are ways of arguing this in court, from the landlord's perspective using the law of property, but they are not clear-cut. The image and the copyright always remain the property of the artist; copyright law by itself ensures that anything an individual inscribes anywhere is their intellectual property, which extends to books, to-do lists and graffiti.

The point is much less about individual rights than it is about making art divested of the notion of ownership. The thing that strikes terror in the dark heart of capitalism is that street art transcends private property: it uses the inert physicality of buildings as the canvases for truly public works of art. Copyright of intellectual property aside – which one assumes Banksy himself holds in a state of willing dispensation – if a Banksy belongs to anyone, it belongs to everyone, and it can only be removed through some gruelling democratic process which is directed towards the public good. A simple-minded claim to ownership of the canvas, regardless of any overt intention as regards the intellectual property thereon, is not enough demolish the public nature of the mural.

The second issue concerns authenticity. Banksy established a company, Pest Control, which authenticates prints and paintings attributed to him, but it does not authenticate murals, which are generally *supposed* to be by Banksy. As such, Stealing Banksy? has no mechanism by which it can guarantee buyers are purchasing a genuine Banksy. In the world of fine art sales, even a universally held supposition is no replacement for a certificate of authenticity supplied by the artist or their representative. Indeed, it is reckless to attempt to sell a work for which you have not secured authenticity, without which the work is practically worthless.

The problem cuts deeper still when we consider that an alleged Banksy is generally supposed to be authentic for as long as it remains on the wall, which is why Pest Control does not authenticate them. But when it is removed to be sold on, the fact that money is about to change hands dictates that it must be authenticated as the genuine article. While it is on the wall, the fact that it looks like a Banksy is enough, but once off the wall and on the market for £200,000, the gap between looking like a Banksy and actually being a Banksy needs to be closed. If it is the former, then the price would be somewhat less than £200,000, if anything at all. In this sense, economic value is decided by authenticity because there is doubt present:

the price depends upon the work genuinely being what the seller professes it to be. Stealing Banksy? bypasses the conventional apparatus of the artworld, so has no way of authenticating the works, and therefore has no recourse to set a reasonable estimate for auction.

The market has a crucial role to play here, since it has the resources to authenticate works of art prior to sale, which can be a difficult and costly process. One aspect of the market that is little discussed is its role as gatekeeper, whereby in authenticating works it is ensuring the integrity of art and artists remains intact by controlling the flow, and sometimes policing the exchange, of fakes. Moreover, the market sends a strong message when it does encounter a fake – no price, no sale and a word with the authorities, which builds confidence in scrupulous dealers and fear in the unscrupulous ones. Authenticity is thus a key indicator of economic value, and represents one way in which the market plays a positive role in the artworld.

In the final analysis, once street art is for sale, the core meaning of the artform begins to wither. It is important to recognise a semantic difference between the mural that has been extracted from the wall and the one that is still on the wall: part of the meaning, as Banksy and practically every other street artist will testify, is the site-specific nature of the work; the precise location – that building, on that street, in that town – forms part of what the work expresses. Once it is removed from that wall, it becomes divorced from that meaning for ever, and, as such, is a shadow of the work Banksy created.

This has implications for cultural value. Part of the reason people will value the mural will be the meaning they suppose it to have in virtue of its being in that particular location in a neighbourhood or town. This will involve a sense of how and what the artist is trying to convey and how people relate to it in virtue of their being bound by that specific location. This site-specific nature of the mural is the locus of its value to or in a culture. That is, its cultural value clearly diminishes considerably, if not disappears entirely, the moment it is lifted off the wall.

The semantic content of the location is something intended by the artist and, as such, is part of the intellectual property of the image, which is legally a distinct entity from the wall that is merely the canvas. As such, the location is not something that can be changed without thereby changing the meaning of the work, which is an infringement of copyright and intellectual property. Even if we deny this interpretation concerning loss of meaning, we still have to answer the claim that the image and the canvas are separate entities, legally owned by different parties, and therefore we have to find a way to transfer the right to intellectual property to the owner of the wall. Here is why authentication is so important: once off the wall, the mural loses much of its cultural value which then jeopardises economic value; the price must reflect that deficiency, so the only thing that can make up for that considerable loss is a certification of authenticity. It is clear, then, economic value, if a work is deemed to be authentic, can follow quite organically from cultural value. It is this that explains how objects can possess inherent economic value, for the fact of authenticity gives a degree of value, not just to art but to anything, regardless of the thing's other features.

The Value of an Idea in the Mind of Someone Living

Questions of authenticity arose when Damien Hirst's company, Science Ltd, became embroiled in a protracted dispute over the right to sell an early site-specific Spot Painting. In this case, it is the economic value of an idea which is at stake, where that idea bears no important relation to its realisation as an artefact. Therefore, cultural value is not relevant here, since it is assured insofar as a Spot Painting, as discussed previously, has the cultural value that is appropriate to it. In the end, Hirst commanded the destruction of the work, confirming the artist's authority as the architect of ideas, which is the final arbiter of value, even for art in the age of minimum wage of reproduction.

The Spot Painting, *Bombay Mix* (1988), was painted directly onto the wallpaper in the backroom of a house in Fulham as a birthday gift from his parents to Jamie Ritblat. When Jess and Roger Simpson bought the house in 2005 they thought they spied an opportunity to make a few hundred thousand, so they had the painting professionally removed, mounted on an aluminium backing board and framed. The cruel twist here is that in the interim Ritblat had returned to Science the work's certificate of authenticity and exchanged it for a work on canvas.

The Simpsons were unprepared for a blunt collision with the complexities of the artworld: according to standard procedure, the owner of a site-specific work is the holder of the certificate, so the Simpsons had no claim of ownership and therefore no right to sell it because they did not possess the certificate. It is the authority of the certificate, as the arbiter of authenticity, that was missing in the Banksy case, so the Simpsons and Stealing Banksy? are in superficially similar situations. However, things pan out rather differently. Science first asked for the piece to be returned and later requested that it be destroyed, since, they claimed, the object is utterly worthless without the certificate. The Simpsons, who professed no affection for Hirst and little interest in art, wondered why Science would want to destroy this artwork and why they were not able to sell it.

The complexity here lies in two areas, both of which have profound emotional resonance, but neither of which offers a solution to this peculiarly aesthetic problem. First, there is an historical case which suggests that the work must remain in situ and nobody has the right to sell it. BBC Arts Editor Will Gompertz, points out that this artwork is a product of its time and all its meaning and value resides in its being there on that wall[50]. Indeed, since the wall paintings series of Spots are amongst the earliest, their cultural significance is in their position in a narrative that has defined a generation; moreover, they are considerably rarer than their brethren on canvas, not least because although they fit in to the Pharmaceutical series, aesthetically speaking, they are the few exceptions whose titles are not named after medications[51].

The second point derives from the old adage that possession is nine tenths of the law. On this view, it is easy to sympathise with the Simpsons' view that the painting is rightfully their property to dispose of as they wish: they legitimately acquired it in the purchase of their house, which was sold according to certain contractual conditions that did not exclude the right to claim ownership over internal walls. But it seems Science's view derives from Robert Nozick, who said, 'justice in holdings is historical; it depends upon what

---

[50] BBC News, 'Row over sale of Hirst spot painting in London house', 14 July 2014.
[51] See Chapter 1 for more on the Spot Paintings.

actually has happened'[52]. This means that the right to possession depends upon a factual examination of a sequence of events, so that, although the Simpsons justly acquired the property, a certain other – historically prior – contract dictates that Science, possessor of the all-important certificate, is the rightful owner of the artwork. However, Science and the Simpsons are at cross purposes: the Simpsons are talking about an object, something they have extracted from the wallpaper, whereas Science is talking about an idea, a concept which is enshrined, not in the makings on the wall, but in the certificate. It is, then, a debate about who is the rightful owner of the concept rather than of any contingent realisation of it.

On the one hand, since site-specific works sometimes have an ephemeral nature, the important thing is that we can situate it in the endless story of the Spot Paintings, so nothing – historically speaking – hangs upon its actually being there in that bedroom in Fulham for ever. On the other hand, discussions about history and possession miss the mark by a wide margin: it is not about tangible things at all, but is rather about ideas, for the valuable thing here is the idea of the Spot Painting that the certificate instantiates, and the value of that idea is independent of any object in reality.

This sounds similar to the Banksy case, where there was a question mark over the authenticity of a painting extracted from a wall, but it differs in the key respect that the Hirst – whether it is on or off the wall – is definitely worthless without the certificate, for it is the idea that constitutes the artwork. Authenticity is here the basis of both cultural and economic value because the certificate confirms that it is a genuine Hirst Spot Painting, giving economic value as a Hirst. At the same

---

[52] Robert Nozick, *Anarchy, State, and Utopia* (New York: Basic Books, 1974), 151.

time, the certificate confirms that the work painted onto that particular wall is the real deal, so, when it was on the wall, the historical fact of its genesis gave it cultural value as one of the early wall-based Spot works. The Simpsons, however, were only interested in economic value, so they were bound to misconstrue the case that Science was presenting to them.

The hallmark of an authentic Hirst is the presence of an idea, since Hirst, by his own admission and by all reasonable interpretations, is a conceptual artist. This is precisely why he is able to have assistants make the work for him, since he is the architect and it matters little to the meaning of the art who the builders are. Legend has it that legions of assistants make Butterfly Paintings by randomly sprinkling dead butterflies over glossed canvases, so that Hirst can drop by occasionally to decree which are the good and right ones. As the origin of the concept of the butterfly paintings, although infinitely repeatable by assistants, only he knows whether the butterflies are in the right place. This centrality of ideas is partly what Graw is getting at with the notion of art as cognitive capitalism: the thing that is being exchanged on the open market is less physical commodities than it is ideas, the results of individual persons' intellectual and creative labours that could not occur by any other means.

As a conceptual artist, Hirst is the architect of ideas whose mere pronouncement over an object is enough to render it an authentic (or inauthentic) work of art[53]. It is for this reason that *Bombay Mix* came with a certificate – anyone can paint a grid of spots on a wall, but only Damien Hirst can render that simple idea an authentic work of Damien Hirst's art and a chapter in the living history of contemporary art. As

---

[53] For a more detailed and critical exploration of Hirst, see Chapter V, We Need to Talk about Damien.

such, Hirst is right to command the destruction of the object in the Simpsons' possession, for he has the requisite authority over the idea, which is contingently instantiated in an object, but which has no necessary connection to it. And whilst everyone can have a say about an object, only one person can make proclamations about an idea.

The Birth of Value out of the Spirit of Experts

In 2014, Sotheby's was sued over the misattribution of a painting which experts later identified as a genuine Caravaggio. The case offers an insight into the relationship between aesthetic qualities and value, revealing that aesthetics has no role to play in judgements of authenticity. It also tangentially poses a challenge to Nietzsche's great dictum that 'it is only as an aesthetic phenomenon that existence and the world are eternally justified'[54].

The painting in question, bought for £140 in 1962, was inherited by Lancelot Thwaytes, who sold it for £42,000 in 2006. It was thought to be the work of an obscure, near-contemporary follower of Caravaggio, but Thwaytes requested that Sotheby's verified this before the sale. Sotheby's, Thwaytes later claimed in court, only conducted x-ray tests, concluding that the painting was an inferior copy of Caravaggio's *The Cardsharps* (c1594), which is held in the collection of the Kimball Museum, Texas. Thwaytes sold the painting to the renowned art historian and collector, Sir Denis Mahon, who had the artwork cleaned and subjected to infrared imaging, which proved that it is in fact a genuine Caravaggio.

---

[54] Friedrich Nietzsche, *The Birth of Tragedy*, trans. Walter Kauffman, in *The Basic Writings of Nietzsche* (New York: Modern Library, 2000), § 5.

Thwaytes, who did not dispute the attribution, then sued Sotheby's for negligence, claiming that the auction house failed in its duty to take all reasonable steps to ensure authenticity[55]. The painting, following Mahon's pronouncement, was valued at £10,000,000.

This is one of art history's miraculous transformation stories in which technology and expert opinion transfigure an insignificant painting into a missing link in the great narrative of art history. At one moment, the painting is an inferior copy of a Caravaggio work by a doting follower, and the next it is a long-lost masterpiece by the man himself. The only change, of course, is that the artist who made the work now has a name, and by some remarkable contingency that name is 'Caravaggio', which means that the painting is worth considerably more than it was before. What has not changed, however, is that it is still as good or as bad a picture as it ever was, since it still possesses the same aesthetic qualities as it did before.

The fact that an attribution of authorship can change the fate and worth of an artwork so dramatically without any change in aesthetic qualities reveals something about the creation of value in art. In the radical absence of the artist or the living machinery of the artist's brand, dead artists' prices depend upon the weight of art history. This is marshalled by experts whose opinions, based largely on historical facts and scientific analysis, seem to change the nature of objects. These experts' power to create great value where before there was none resides in scholarship and learning, but, used within the market and outside of their academies, it feels like conjuring.

---

[55] In January 2015, the High Court ruled in favour of Sotheby's, concluding it had taken all reasonable steps to fulfil its duty to authenticate the work prior to sale. Thwaytes was ordered to pay at least £1,800,000 to Sotheby's.

Economic value has materialised out of a pronouncement on authenticity, whereby nothing has changed, and yet everything is different from before. Economic value is following cultural value, but the dynamic is odd because cultural value, which would usually be fixed by history and authenticity, has undergone a dramatic change and thus precipitated the fluidity of economic value.

That experts have this power is integral to their being experts, but it also betrays the strange frisson between art as culture and art as economics. In art critical discourse, we refer to aesthetic qualities as the grounds of our judgements about the work's cultural value. This is a matter, philosophically speaking, of the work having certain properties – like serenity, grace or elegance – which are the perceptual grounds of the experiences that inform our judgements. Even if, in a pre-theoretical mindset, we do not articulate it this way, aesthetics is the foundation of our commerce with art, so it is peculiar – if not disconcerting – that these experts, who are after all exemplary aestheticians, are called upon to ignore aesthetics in favour of history and science.

The Thwaytes vs Sotheby's case demonstrates that although aesthetic qualities are essential to cultural value, they are irrelevant to economic value in cases where authenticity is disputed. Aesthetic qualities have nothing to do with the identity of the artist, the position of the work in art history or its provenance, which are the bedrock of how authenticity is assured on the secondary market. The experts are there to establish these things beyond reasonable doubt. The aesthetic qualities of *The Cardsharps* remains unchanged from the moment that Thwaytes inherited it to the moment Mahon announced his discovery. And yet, unbelievable economic value has been created without recourse to aesthetics, the very thing that is the locus of the work's cultural value.

This situation is disastrous on two levels. First, by locating the relevance of aesthetic qualities in cultural value alone it divorces it from its causally efficacious role in determining economic value, rendering the latter a mere affectation of historical contingency. And second, it abandons Nietzsche's dictum with which we began, since the artwork is no longer justified as an aesthetic phenomenon, but as an historical one. While there is no heresy in abandoning Nietzsche, there is a serious problem if money trumps the very thing that eternally justifies the pursuit of art. Once art becomes an object whose value is justified by historical facts over aesthetic qualities, it loses the very distinction that makes it both culturally worthwhile and economically exceptional.

The question then becomes, are we willing to accept this considerable diminishment of the importance of cultural value in order to secure the integrity of authenticity? The answer has to be yes because authenticity matters in a very fundamental way, not just to the market but to anyone who takes art seriously. On the one hand, we appreciate art as the products of individual human beings, so it matters whether a work is by the hand of Caravaggio or not; and on the other hand, a false claim to authenticity is tantamount to a lie, and nobody likes being lied to. In fact, it is not the case that cultural value ceases to matter in cases where authenticity is disputed, since although nothing has changed aesthetically, the mere fact that *The Cardsharps* fills a gap in the Caravaggio narrative is part of its newfound cultural value. This will affect the economic value, for sure, but only after authenticity has been confirmed.

The Ursprung *of Modern Art*[56]

Artworks sometimes possess cultural value in virtue of their precise position in the narrative of art history. A work's being made at a certain moment in time can entail that it is culturally significant, and therefore cherished and revered, because history itself – the mere fact of a work's being made at a particular point in time and then its having trickle-down art historical consequences – creates cultural value. History, so construed, impinges upon economic value in numerous ways, not least in the sense that a work's historic importance can tend to render it truly priceless, but that shall not be our concern here. Instead, we are concerned with how history itself produces cultural value in a parallel way to how authenticity produces economic value – that is, organically and logically.

Consider Marcel Duchamp's *Fountain* (1917): as an object, it is not much to look at and might even be thought crass, but through the historical narrative of the dawn of the readymade and its struggle for recognition, the work is transformed into a wonder of art history. The cultural value of the work is, however, even greater than the standard narrative admits. *Fountain* broods quietly in a corner of Tate Modern; it knows that you valorise it and it knows that you do not know the half of it. Duchamp's *Fountain* is not quite what it seems, and for that very reason it is more important and ground-breaking than we ordinarily imagine, for not only did it revolutionise the

---

[56] The German word *Ursprung* has two pertinent senses: 'cradle', as in that in which something is nurtured, and 'fountain', from which something springs forth. Duchamp's *Fountain* is both the cradle of modern art and – literally and figuratively – the fountain from which springs the enterprise of 20th Century philosophical aesthetics.

concept of art, but it also prefigured the way in which art became a commodity on the modern market. Almost all of its value is cultural. This immense cultural value surpasses any price that could be put upon it, and yet the precise details of its history are little known.

The basic story is well known. In 1917, Duchamp bought a standard Bedfordshire model urinal from a New York ironmongers' store. Struck by the aesthetic of this everyday utilitarian object, he turned it on its back, signed it, 'R Mutt 1917', in black marker and submitted it to the Society of Independent Artists open exhibition. The committee, of which Duchamp was a member, rejected the work, despite the fact that the only condition for inclusion was payment of the $6 entry fee, which R Mutt had done.

Duchamp remained quiet about R Mutt's identity and watched as a fierce debate raged: it was thought indecent and an affront to the nobility of fine art, being as it was an everyday bathroom appliance. It is difficult now to imagine, still less to empathise with, the outrage, but at that moment, nothing like it had been done before. In some versions of the story, eternally unconfirmed, the work was included in the exhibition, hidden behind a screen as a half-hearted concession to the Society's democratic principles. In any case, the public never set eyes on it.

The next chapter in the story is perhaps lesser known. An undefeated and good-humoured Duchamp could not let this work – which he, after all, thought to be a cataclysmic breakthrough – go unnoticed, so he took *Fountain* to be photographed by Alfred Stieglitz. The picture was published in avant-garde magazine *The Blind Man*, along with a letter from Stieglitz and articles by artist Beatrice Wood and art collector Walter Arensberg, having already been gleefully publicised by the New York Dadaists. It was an anonymous editorial, believed to have been written by Wood (who was, incidentally, in love with Duchamp), that spelled out the artistic revolution. The editorial stated: 'Whether Mr Mutt made the fountain with his own hands or not has no importance. He CHOSE it. He took an article of life, placed it so that its useful significance disappeared under the new title and point of view - created a new thought for that object'[57].

And here one story ends while another begins. Art would never be the same again; the river of creativity had burst its banks, flooding the cultural landscape with the possibility of a new art. Practically everyone in art today, theorists and practitioners alike, owes some debt to Duchamp, even though it is so entrenched in the canon now that we hardly consider it with more than a vague sigh. Two interconnected things happened: one, art was liberated from the mimesis paradigm in which it had been locked for so long – art no longer had to imitate reality, it could simply *be* reality; and two, in virtue of that, the boundaries for what could be art, and therefore the very definition of 'art', had been widened, never again to be narrowed[58].

The effect of *Fountain* was both radical and slow-burning. On the one hand, it sent waves from New York to Europe, questioning the limits of art itself, which was defined academically by painting and sculpture, and still just trapped in a paradigm of mimesis. Duchamp's great coup was to move art

---

[57] Marcel Duchamp, Henri Pierre Roche and Beatrice Wood (eds), *The Blind Man: New York Dada,* 1917 (New York: Ugly Duckling Press, 2017). This is a centenary reissue of the two volumes of the ground-breaking journal, volume 2 of which contains the reactions to *Fountain.*

[58] For more on these two points, art as mimesis and the definition of art, see Arthur C Danto, *After the End of Art* (Princeton: Princeton University Press, 1998), 29 and 46 respectively.

away from traditional notions of craft and mimesis, and towards art as an intellectual, rather than purely visual, exercise. *Fountain* thus began conceptual art.

On the other hand, although *Fountain* was the breaking point for art, it would take the best part of fifty years for the face of art to change completely. It was not until art had passed through surrealism, Cubism and abstract expressionism that it would reach its terminal crisis: Clement Greenberg's vision of pure modernist painting as the saviour of art ground to a halt, leaving a void which ultimately was filled with minimalism and pop art. Indeed, once abstract expressionism had faded, Greenberg felt art and himself to be redundant, consequently giving up criticism and living the rest of his days on the back of his reputation alone. It was at this point, when abstract expressionism died and the pure pale of painting had been exhausted, that pop art emerged, hailing a new era of art in which the everyday was transfigured into art, which Danto calls 'the transfiguration of the commonplace'[59]. But Duchamp was the catalyst for the pop artists who levered art out of a defunct modernism; he was the immediate precursor to the anything goes, post-historical conceptually driven artworld that Danto would eventually characterise as 'the end of art'[60].

The major breakthrough, and that which redefined art philosophically, is that the readymade was born with *Fountain*. Duchamp thus provided a fresh challenge to agitated efforts to philosophically describe the nature of art, since, at the turn of the century, philosophers turned their attention away from questions of beauty and towards the definition of art itself. But the principal philosophers engaged in the task of definition –

---

[59] Arthur C Danto, *The Transfiguration of the Commonplace* (Cambridge: Harvard University Press, 1981).
[60] See Danto, *After the End of Art,* Chapters 1 and 2.

Clive Bell, RG Collingwood and William E Kennick – were still primarily dealing with visual art narrowly construed as painting, sculpture and drawing along the lines of the mimesis paradigm; namely art that attempted to represent or imitate reality, figurative art, if you will[61]. *Fountain* thus presented a challenge to philosophical definitions – how this object could be a work of art could not be comfortably subsumed under any answer to the question of what art it is. It was not until the 1960s, with Danto's theory of the Artworld or Dickie's Institutional Theory, that *Fountain* found a place in philosophy and retroactively became the starting point for a new philosophical aesthetics[62].

R Mutt's intervention has another, much less widely known, chapter with a much more surprising consequence. There are 17 versions of *Fountain,* 15 of which survive today, the original having been discarded as quotidian rubbish. It was not until 1950, however, that Duchamp sanctioned a copy of the original for an exhibition in New York; he did the same in Paris in 1953, which went missing, and in Stockholm in 1963. Then, in 1964, Duchamp permitted his Milan gallerist, Arturo Schwarz, to produce an edition of 8, with 2 artist's proofs, 2 exhibition copies and 1 prototype model. All 16 are exact replicas of the original Bedfordshire model urinal, with the signature of R Mutt reproduced in black paint. It may come as a surprise to some that artefact in the Tate Modern – the archetypal readymade – is a *sculpture* of an everyday object, fabricated by artisans, and a not found object at all.

---

[61] Clive Bell, *Art* (London: Dodo Press, 1913); RG Collingwood, *The Principles of Art* (London: Oxford University Press, 1938); William E Kennick, 'Does Traditional Aesthetics Rest on a Mistake?', *Mind*, vol. 67, no. 267 (July 1958) 317-334.

[62] Danto, 'The Artworld' and George Dickie, *Art and the Aesthetic: An Institutional Analysis* (Ithaca, NY: Cornell University Press, 1974).

This move towards reproducible works of art that could, in theory at least, be reproduced indefinitely, marked a change in the attitude towards the work of art as cultural product. The fact that Duchamp sanctioned a copy as and when it was needed, not placing any especial value on the original or limiting the edition to an absolute finite number, as would have been previously done with sculpture, indicates a moment at which the artwork ceases to be precious as a unique object. This is what Benjamin is talking about when he says film and photography obliterate the aura of the work of art: an object – a painting or sculpture – is a unique thing that was touched by the hand of the artist and for ever more, as it persists through time, bears that mark of distinction[63]. The result of this for film is Hollywood, but for sculpture the net result is that rather than becoming entirely devalued by reproducibility, sculpture becomes lucrative because each copy is a unit on the market. It opens up the possibility of an indefinite revenue from the artist's product, which is only possible because any given unit has no particular value as a uniquely situated object. Duchamp thus laid the bedrock of the contemporary art market that exchanges readily repeatable copies, and he let Warhol take the credit and Hirst take the blame.

In retrospect, it seems a remarkable coincidence that the bulk of the extant copies of *Fountain* – thirteen of them – were produced in the very same year that Warhol staged his Brillo Box exhibition at New York's Stable Gallery. For Danto, this exhibition in 1964 was the point at which art turned a corner into its post-historical phase where anything, even a mere Brillo Box, could be art. This turning point, which Danto is right to identify as the decisive moment, would not, however, have been possible without Duchamp's founding gesture in

---

[63] Benjamin, 'The Work of Art in the Age of Mechanical Reproduction', § II.

1917. The thing that Danto does not apprehend is the further cataclysm that, in making perfectly life-like copies of everyday utilitarian objects (indiscernibles, Danto calls them), Warhol was finally turning art into a manufactured commodity. Although Duchamp initially ordered exhibition copies of *Fountain*, his permission for his gallerist to produce copies for sale on the open market signalled the commodification of the work, which occurred in parallel with Warhol's somewhat more wholesale approach. A work of art that originated in 1917 begins to feel eerily contemporary once we consider that it prefigured the production and dissemination that characterises a great deal of contemporary commercial art. *Fountain* is the charming simulation of a readymade, which was mass-produced by someone other than the artist in order to be dispersed, carrying with it the illusion of uniqueness and the mythology of its creation.

Duchamp was ahead of his time in 1917, but a stroke of genius in 1950 set the ball rolling for an advance that would change art for ever. He unwittingly invented the value industry by first transfiguring an everyday object into art, giving cultural value to that which is purely utilitarian, and second, by making that gesture indefinitely repeatable so that innumerable instances of economic value could be extracted from the one idea. *Fountain* is a reproduction of a mundane object from the fabric of banality, and at the same time it is anything but that. It is a modern artistic statement, made with an age-old commitment to mimeses, repeated and distributed all over the world. A poet might say that *Fountain*, an imitation of both the real world and itself, turns out to be the first postmodern artwork before modernism had even reached its peak.

The story of modern art is, to a large extent, predicated upon the notion of the readymade, the found object from everyday life transfigured into art. The cultural value of *Fountain* resides in the fact that it was the first such artwork, setting in motion the unfolding history of modern art. In addition, Duchamp compelled philosophers to turn their serious attention to a thoroughgoing redefinition of art, as *Fountain* helped usher in the end of mimesis. And finally, Duchamp was one of the early pioneers of mass-produced sculpture. All these breakthroughs and shockwaves, some of which had immediate effects while others took time to take hold, are down to *Fountain*'s precise position in the narrative of art: just after impressionism, van Gogh and Monet, and just before Picasso, Dali and modernism. In this sense, its cultural value – construed literally as its value to culture – is derived from its precise position in art history, as the First Cause of an entire phase in history. There is no reasonable price for this colossal influence, so cultural value here outruns economic value by more than a few miles.

The more art there is after *Fountain*, the more valuable *Fountain* becomes because everything, in some way, stems from it or is indebted to it. Cultural value is here established by a mere contingency – Duchamp having a particular idea at a moment in time – without any conjuring of the value industry. Indeed, the value of *Fountain* is a result of the historical fact of its creation and little else besides, since the aesthetic is unremarkable, the concept is so well rehearsed by now that it hardly registers, and the myth of its uniqueness is a commonplace misconception. Its influence is so deep and wide that there is nothing the value industry can do to add or subtract value. The value derives, with uniform regularity, from the facts of history: the fact is that Duchamp was in the right place at the right time, and made something that is indispensable for culture and unequivocally priceless on the market. And nobody's opinion could ever change the facts of how influential and therefore significant *Fountain* has been for modern art.

V. Manufacturing Wonder

How money became more famous than art

The value industry's crystallisation and London's maturation as an epicentre of art occurred with the YBAs in the 1990s. For these fortunate and infamous young British artists, the money seemed more famous than the art. It was, if you will, the value industry's post-Warhol second-coming. The YBAs created artworks of immense cultural value, which revitalised and refreshed a dwindling contemporary art scene. The value industry marketed those artefacts, so strange and so alluring, to the general public and the art establishment, in such a way as to treat art as the ultimate commodity and to make the prices, rather than the artworks, headline news.

The YBAs, as we have seen, were at the forefront of both a reinvigorated interest in British art and an unspeakable boom in the contemporary art market, in no small measure creating the artworld we have today. But they were so famous for their riches and celebrity that history has all too easily forgotten that some of them are world-class artists. Chief among the truly great artists of that generation are Tracey Emin and Damien

Hirst, whom you probably think are, at best, all style and no substance, and at worst, charlatans and crooks.

One of the mindbending achievements of the value industry is that during the hubris of the 90s art boom it made such a fuss about money and spectacle that everyone, for a long time, forgot to think about the art. In so doing, it made you associate Emin with awkward emotional exhibitionism and Hirst with stratospheric prices, and by that token it made you forget that they are both important and good artists.

Everything You Steel Will Turn to Ash[64]

The unchecked might of the market can render impotent the museums whose mandate it is to preserve our rich cultural history, so back in 2014 when Saatchi announced he was selling Tracey Emin's iconic *My Bed*, there was a very real fear that market forces and private interests would vanquish culture. Owing to the stretched finances of the Tate Galleries and the sheer lust of the market, the bed seemed likely to drift away on a sea of missed opportunities, vanishing into the clutches of a private collector. This simply would not have been acceptable, since that bed – divisive as it is – is one of the great cultural products of the YBA movement and one of the keenest illustrations of how that era produced some spectacular, and now underrated, art.

Contemporary art captures in unequivocal form the spirit of the moment, acting as both barometer and mirror; it is an enduring document that conveys to future generations a lost past. In the 1990s, Britain got the art it both deserved and

---

[64] I have, for romanticism, preserved Tracey Emin's misspelling.

needed. The YBAs captured a moment in history characterised by sharp economic decline followed by amazing boom, political optimism and a devil-may-care attitude. They struck gold with a relentless project of shock and awe. Dead stuff, bullet wounds, elephant dung, stale kebabs, serial killers, sharks and Nazis caused outrage, and they were all exhilarating spectacles. But Emin stood out from the crowd; she went for the shock and bore of the disarmingly ordinary – handwritten letters, drawings, hand-sewn upholstered chairs, ink drawings, quilts, and unmade beds. The horror was in the sheer banality of the artefacts and the ongoing narrative of one woman's tumultuous emotional life. Emin's work was personal and human, unlike her peers, who were dealing with the big issues of life and death, and so it became an ongoing autobiography of how one woman grew up and battled to survive the ravages of life. It could have been anyone's story, but it happened to have been Tracey Emin's. The brilliance of her work lies in its humanity, its authenticity, its unwavering faithfulness to the rawness of the human condition, and her astute sense of materiality.

Amid smouldering headlines and fading memories, the art of the Nineties is typified by That Shark and That Bed precisely because they crystallised a moment. *My Bed,* in particular, signalled a shift in emphasis: the Duchampian readymade lost its clean, almost inhuman surface and became the detritus of a life lived in peril. Suddenly contemporary art was about humanity again, not as an abstract collective, as it is in the work of Hirst or the Chapman Brothers, but comprised of striving individuals, now elevated to the status of celebrity, but at their core mere struggling mortals. This is precisely the kind of moment in art history that a culture should revere and preserve: the moment when the art that was all about spectacle and shock suddenly reveals that beneath the surface there is just the bare suffering of human individuals.

The value industry, in its pursuit of a reliable product, had come to rely on the clean, manufactured aesthetic of the YBAs: Gary Hume's glossy, hard-edged paintings, Gavin Turk's bronze casts, Hirst's cabinets. Then Emin came along with something which turned that upside down because the bed demonstrated an apparent lack of effort in craftmanship. After all, even if Hirst's shark was not convincing as art, it was possible to conceive of its value as an artefact, since the effort and expense required to acquire a tiger shark and encase it in a tank of formaldehyde suggested a value all of its own, whereas the bed was just a bed and, as such, worth nothing in the eyes of anybody except Emin. The value industry had to create value out of myth and press coverage because the object could not do the work itself.

My Bed works on two levels: it is a self-portrait of Mad Tracey from Margate losing her mind in a Waterloo council flat, and it is an antidote to the glamorous veneer of contemporary art. It was both similar to and different from the art of 1998 insofar as it was typically YBA in its celebration of the grotesque and its inevitable courtship of media scrutiny; but the purity of its emotional register was refreshing, as it was uncommonly self-reflective for that generation. *My Bed* is a great work of art partly because it enforces this art historical shift in its own socio-historic context, but also because – no matter what can be written about it – the lived experience of the work effortlessly generates rich emotional and intellectual responses. Love it or hate it, *My Bed* does that thing that art is supposed to do – it forces the audience to respond on *both* the levels of thought *and* feeling; and this happens in virtue of *aesthetics*, since it is the way the work looks and feels that ultimately provokes the response with only a tangential contribution from its broader context. Emin is a great aesthetician in the sense that she knows how to manipulate materiality in order to provoke responses, which is a skill so many artists lack, and it is for this reason that *My Bed* is and remains one of the great artworks of the 20th Century.

The bed's cultural value was bolstered by its controversy. Each new media storm and each new *Daily Mail* reader exclaiming, 'That's not art! My five-year-old could do better!' generated publicity and brought the work to a wider and wider audience, whose aesthetic sensibilities were being awakened and challenged, proving again and again that it functions perfectly as a work of art. And, of course, it was this immense cultural value which seemed so perilously at stake when Saatchi decided to sell it on the open market. However, its economic value had a somewhat rockier road to travel from its first private sale to its eventual offering on the secondary market. Throughout the 90s, Emin had refused to sell to Saatchi because of his role in Margaret Thatcher's rise to power[65]. But shortly after the 1999 Turner Prize, Emin, who did not win the coveted prize, agreed to meet Saatchi at a café on Cork Street. Suddenly famous and possessing some sway, Emin cut a shrewd deal with the revered collector: she agreed sell *My Bed* to Saatchi, via her New York gallery Lehmann Maupin, for £150,000 only if he also bought a beach hut, titled *The Last Thing I Said to You is Don't Leave Me Here* (1997), for £75,000. In September 2000, both works were shown at Saatchi's Boundary Road gallery.

---

[65] Charles Saatchi's advertising firm, Saatchi & Saatchi, which he ran with his brother, Maurice, spearheaded the Conservative Party's 1979 election campaign, which brought Margaret Thatcher to Downing Street. See Fendley, *Commercial Break*, Chapter 4.

The beach hut sadly perished in the Great Fire of Momart, along with much of Saatchi's collection[66]. The bed, however, was spared the flames because Saatchi had it lovingly installed in a spare bedroom of his Kensington home. He refused, in true Saatchi style, to lend it to the Hayward for its monumental 2011 Emin retrospective, so until it appeared on the block at Christie's King Street saleroom, it had not been seen in the UK since it was displayed at the Scottish National Gallery of Modern Art in 2008.

When the moment finally came, Christie's estimate for *My Bed* was a modest £800,000 to £1,200,000. It seemed a preposterous price for a seminal, iconic work, but it reflected the fact that Emin's secondary market record – for another bed, *To Meet My Past* (2002), also sold by Saatchi – was at that time £481,875. Whilst £1,200,000 is peanuts for a billionaire collector, who would happily see the bidding into eight figures, it was too much for the nation and far beyond the means of the Tate. It looked, rather glibly, as if the market ruled supreme: the first time the work ever appeared on the open market, it was only within the reach of private collectors. In one of her appliquéd blankets, Emin says 'everything you steel will turn to ash', and it seemed as if that was a prophecy for the bed's fate: stolen from the nation by one collector after another, it will be consumed by the raging fire of the market and the state's museums will be unable to extinguish the blaze.

When the hour finally arrived, the crowds spilled out of the doors of the saleroom and extended across the banks of

---

[66] Charlotte Higgins and Vikram Dodd, '50 Years of British Art Lies in Ashes', *The Guardian,* 27 May 2004. Momart is an art storage company based in Leyton, East London, where much of Saatchi's collection was kept in storage. Among the works lost in the fire was Emin's tent, *Everyone I Have Ever Slept With 1963-1995* (1995).

telephone bidders, comprising 190 bidders from 28 countries[67]. But amid the saleroom's unique blend of tension and joviality, something more than the sale of luxury goods was happening. Brett Gorvy, at the time Christie's international head of post-war and contemporary art, summed it up as a 'very discerning element to this market...People are really making distinct choices. It's a very subjective response to works'. Read that again. It is completely meaningless. Rather, Gorvy was trying to say: 'Of course, we have some very important works for sale tonight, but it's all about money.'

In a sense, Christie's is in the business of dispensing fragments of art history into the hands of custodians. The fact that money exchanges hands here tells us about the nature of social relations that demand compensation for goods and services rendered, but it tells us nothing about the immanent nature of the artwork, only that a private individual is willing to pay x amount to claim ownership of a particular object y. As it happened, on that Tuesday night at Christie's there were significant works of art which required no additional help to assure their cultural value.

The interesting thing about auction houses is that they are art historically grounded in the sense that they create value through the seemingly objective science of historical provenance. That is, by listing all previous owners of the work, and documenting their collections, and noting where and how each careful owner had acquired the work, the auction house is, on the one hand, assuring buyers that the work is genuine, since it has been legitimately bought and sold before, and on the other hand, signalling that the work is eminently desirable, since it has been held in esteemed collections. As such, they are dealing in a form of mythology: the creation of cultural

---

[67] Christie's, London, 1 July 2014.

value out of narratives that employ tangible human histories, which are documented, dated and archived, evidenced for all to see but no less mythologised for it.

At the time, the sales talk about town was of a 'return to painting', an historical move, palpably evidenced by the market, away from conceptual art and back towards the steady dynamism of the canvas, with major pieces by Jean Dubuffet, Jenny Saville and Hurvin Anderson. Of course, this was only happening in the sale room, outside of which there was no such thing as a return to painting, since there had never been any departure from it. Painting was, as it is and always has been, an ever-present staple. The very sound of a 'return to painting' was enough, however, to grease the wheels of buyers' spending inclinations; a sort of instant mythology which justified surprising prices and intellectualised something rather frankly ordinary. Nowhere was this more apparent than with Peter Doig, who was tipped to take Hirst's crown as Britain's most expensive living artist. When the Doig came up, the room was gripped: after the bids came thick and fast, creeping ever closer to victory, it went for £9,900,000, leaving King Damien intact. The return to paining, always an economic conceit with cultural undertones, remained incomplete.

The highlight of the night was Lot 19. From Emin's point of view, it was the end of an era; she had to let go of the piece that made her career and send it, like a grown child, out into the world to fend for itself. *My Bed* tells the story of the breakup of a relationship; it is a self-portrait that contains the very grit of the artist's soul. And that is precisely what you feel when you stand before it – a snapshot of a moment in time, a slice of a real human life that expresses raw emotion in a surprisingly elegant piece of a sculpture. And a couple of heated minutes in a crowded saleroom were to decide the fate of the last great artwork of the 20th Century.

The bidding began, in an atmosphere of controlled hysteria, at £650,000. Then, after a barrage of bids taking it comfortably above its high estimate, it suddenly faltered around £1,800,000: perhaps only for a second – one of those seconds that are so pregnant with anticipation that they stretch beyond man and time – the frenzy abated when the room took a moment to consider the gravity of it all. Some people dropped out, everyone held their breath, and the auctioneer, Jussi Pylkkänen, filled one final dramatic pause by turning directly to Emin to say, in theatrical tones, 'not yours Tracey'. And then in a flash it was gone for more than double its high estimate at £2,546,500. Emin shrieked and everyone applauded. The moment had passed in spectacular style.

It is a lot of money for an unmade bed, for sure, but of course it is not just an unmade bed. It is the culmination of an art historical tradition descended from Rembrandt's self-portraits, sieved through Duchamp and forged in the furnace of the great art boom of the 90s and New Labour's manufactured optimism. *The Guardian* newspaper reported that the bed had been bought by Emin's dealer, Jay Jopling, and everything suddenly seemed right with the world[68]. Jopling's hands, we thought, are as good as any for the care of this great work, since he, in a sense, nurtured it in its early years. But all was not as it seemed.

The idea that commercial galleries do not sell to just anyone, but select their clients very carefully, sounds like outright elitism. It sounds as if they deliberately seek out the rich and powerful, latch on to fashion-following celebrities and

---

[68] Hannah Ellis-Petersen, 'Tracey Emin's Bed is sold at auction for over £2,500,000', *The Guardian*, 1 July 2014.

always ensure a good deal for their friends. It is true that simply being able to afford it is not an immediate pass to walking into a gallery and buying an artwork, but there is a more refined logic to it than this suggests. The artwork gains a certain kudos from being in the right hands, which becomes a part of its value.

The excitement over Emin's *My Bed* reached a surprising climax when it was revealed that Jay Jopling had secured the work on behalf of a client, Cologne-based super-collector Count Christian Duerckheim. There is no doubt that Count Duerckheim is an important collector: his collection includes entire swathes of work that document the careers of Georg Baselitz, Gerhard Richter and Sigmar Polke with a depth and breadth that tell the story of modern German art. Count Duerckheim, like many of the artists he collects, is a refugee of the Second World War, who watched the bombing of Dresden from a stalled train; as such, his collection is an exploration of the aftermath of the darkest period in European history. In a sense, all the works in his collection form a personal and historical narrative, which speaks as much about the collector as about his collection. As such, the works accrue value from being in this collection because they are knitted into a narrative that ties together the universal appeal of art – as culture, as aesthetics – to the particular value of art to an individual human subject. The value industry creates this situation with its discerning approach to placing works in collections so that such cultural value may later translate into economic value. After all, some part of the bed's value at auction was derived, first, from the fact that it was the first time the work was available on the open market, and second, from the fact it had been in the collection of Saatchi, godfather of the YBAs.

Count Duerckheim said he bought *My Bed* because 'it is a metaphor for life, where troubles begin and logics die'[69], thus simultaneously burrowing to the heart of the work's meaning and effortlessly slotting it in to the theme of his collection. It did not matter in the end, to either Count Duerckheim or anyone else, how much the bed sold for. *My Bed* is an example of an artwork which transcends its press attention, price and mythology to stand out as a truly great work of art. The thing that Count Duerckheim was conscious of, and that many others may miss, is that he had acquired an item of cultural value which occupies a significant place in art history.

The initial controversy over the bed, staged at length and very publicly throughout the gruelling 1999 Turner Prize, and any subsequent media attention Emin attracted for either her art or her outspoken ideas, had a double-blind effect: on the one hand, it created the cultural value of her work by weaving an ever-increasingly complex web of mythology; and on the other hand, it blinded people to that cultural value because all they could see was the myth, the hysteria, the madness of Mad Tracey from Margate. This was the story with the YBAs in general – economic value and mass media generated a mythology that obscured the reality of cultural value.

If there was ever any doubt about the bed, standing before Emin's tiny paintings in the vast galleries of White Cube Bermondsey resolved all such doubts for ever. In the autumn following the sale of the bed, Emin opened her first major solo show in London in five years, where it became clear how Emin, no matter what she does, explicates the entire

---

[69] Maev Kennedy, 'Tracey Emin's bed returns to Tate', *The Guardian*, 29 July 2014.

reason for art's existence[70]. Every line is a snatch of emotion, every drip a careful meditation, equal parts memory and fantasy, conveyed by artist to audience in an act of pure communication. Emin will never be Baselitz or Kahlo, but nor would she want to be. She just wants to touch your soul, even though you think she is an irritating emotional exhibitionist. But you are wrong. Tracey Emin is the perfect artist, and she is giving you exactly what you want, even if you are too stuck in the Nineties to see it.

Emin is the victim of the myth that she necessarily had to perpetuate in order to be understood: the image of Mad Tracey from Margate is the basically true but wilfully exaggerated foundation on which her art is contextualised. Emin transfigures a lost past into a living present, blurring the line between life and art until it is about nothing other than humanity. If you shut out the noise from the myth of Mad Tracey, you will see why she is precisely the kind of artist that you really want. Paradoxically, Emin is both an archetypal product of the value industry and an anathema to it: she is a media-friendly myth machine, creating cultural value out of the nothingness of the everyday, and yet her work rarely achieves an economic value that it seems worthy of.

Emin embodies the very things that people so often complain are missing from contemporary art, namely craft, expression and narrative. In a world where art is manufactured to order, never touched by artists' hands, studded with diamonds, resembles industrial products of little obvious value and insists on some high-minded conceptual grounding, Emin is a breath of fresh air. She treats art as the hand-made expression of her inner being, as if she is using all the

---

[70] Tracey Emin, 'The Last Great Adventure is You', White Cube Bermondsey, London, 8 October – 16 November 2014.

resources of modernity to make art of a romantic, bygone period that died with van Gogh. Emin treats art as self-expression, as catharsis and as reflection on the wider human condition, which, all the way back to Sophocles, is the central calling of art.

Emin prefers embroidery to machine manufactured sculpture, drawing rather than digital imaging, paintings that are the result of years of contemplation, and even neons cast in her own handwriting from antique Japanese glass. It is not just a romantic attachment to traditional materials and processes, everything is forged by her own hand because she views art as the objective embodiment of the artist's subjective intention. There is a profound respect for the artist's craft as an act of communion with materials and audience alike. Every one of those pencil drawings, monoprints, paintings and gouaches is the laboured fruit of Emin's hand, brought into being from a belief in the necessity of unmediated, personal communication.

There is an immediacy of sensation and feeling in Emin's work, which feels at odds with a world where rampant globalisation has caused art's central motifs to become grand narratives about abstractions. Emin boils the big picture down to the Self; she is an expressionist who explores the richness and vivacity of human emotion; she simultaneously constructs an autobiography and unfurls a rigorous analysis of human drama that contains kernels of truth for everyone. Although the work is always about Emin's life and experiences, there is no pretence that she is so exceptional that none of it is ever felt or experienced by any other human being. We see ourselves in the work because to have these emotions articulated in art is to be given the means to explore them. Paradoxically, those people who cannot deal with the mass-production of Hirst or the stark minimalism of Martin Creed are the very same people who both want to art be everything that Emin is and yet reject her as a person and as an artist.

Emin has often said that she always longed to be a writer. She is a natural storyteller and, as an artist, the story she is telling is that of the life of Tracey Emin. Every piece of work is a chapter in that story, forming a coherent totality, which most artists, still drunk or hungover on postmodernism, eschew in favour of a discursive plot that requires, as Benjamin would say, appreciation in a state of distraction. *My Bed*, for example, is to be contemplated like a portrait, as a unified whole that tells the entire story in one sitting, precisely as Aristotle advises the writer of tragedy to present the unity of an action[71].

Emin principally understands that there is meaning in materiality and uses that – rather than abstract ideas – as the sole bearer of meaning in her art, which makes it easy to read, since the aesthetic and the meaning are one and the same thing. In a work like *Knowing My Enemy* (2002), the wood, peeling paint, mottled glass and faded curtains speak of neglect, lost hope and vulnerability to the elements at the same time as embodying in the very core of their being a secret history imparted by the passing of time. Or her famous blankets that are composed of swatches of fabric culled from her clothes, curtains and furniture, so the materials themselves, as well as the signs and symbols they denote, tell her life story. There is an edifying transparency here, effortlessly achieved through immaculate attention to detail in materiality.

Emin's cultural value lies significantly in the fact that – during the 90s and beyond – she has always treated art as self-expression, which became unfashionable long ago and was

---

[71] 'Unity of action' is Aristotle's way of saying that the artist, in his case, the playwright, should present the whole story at once in such a way that the audience is not left with unanswered questions or loose ends. See Aristotle, *Poetics* (London: Penguin Classics, 1996)

emphatically not what the 90s was about; Emin's self-reflection was too romantic, too neurotic, almost too parochial for the decade of Cool Britannia. Nonetheless, she was and is ultimately fulfilling anyone's best guess at the purpose of art – to edify the human spirit through craft and emotional expression. The value industry, so obsessed with the economic value, does not give Emin enough credit for this exceptional, and yet somehow ordinary, approach to art. Emin is a good example of how the value industry can sideline a culturally significant artist by focusing on mythology because the economics do not stack up.

In the end, this is all you really want from art: pure cultural value burrowing to the heart of what it means to be human and resting in the core of the purpose of art. The gentle touch of the artist's hand, the sincere expression of emotion and a coherent narrative, all embedded in an aesthetic that has the weight of art history behind it and a transparency of meaning within it. A whole life unfolds in Emin's work and sometimes it is ugly, harrowing, and trite, but it is also replete with tenderness and affection, just like your sorry life. There is no conceptual trick, no essential spiritual complexity – there is just anguish, love, loss and joy, which are all things that everybody, even people who read the *Daily Mail*, can understand. If you cannot see and appreciate that in Tracey Emin, then there is nothing anybody can really do for you. And for that very reason, her cultural value is incalculable, no matter what economic value has to say.

We Need to Talk about Damien

Damien Hirst is one of the great artists of the 20th Century, but the value industry has seen to it that hardly anyone would concede it. The very mythology that drove Hirst's prices up has been his downfall: the idea of the superstar artist, born into nothing, growing up in Leeds, making his own way in the artworld via the house of a hoarder and through Goldsmiths College, building an empire, employing hundreds of minions and becoming the most expensive living British artist with work that is nothing more than manufactured repetition, shameless bling and cynical shock tactics. All of this has made Hirst very famous and very wealthy, but it has also rendered many people unable to take him seriously as an artist. Hirst is thus a quintessential example of how economic value, driven by myth, can eclipse cultural value.

We need to talk about Damien because we need to see how the value industry has profited from blinding us to his greatness. The work that best illustrates what is going on at the core of Hirst's practice is *Still* (1994), a stainless steel and glass display cabinet containing glistening surgical instruments. Here is the aesthetic of minimalism effortlessly carrying the weight of a conceptual project which tethers timeless existential themes to contemporary excesses. The enchantment of *Still* lies in the duality of the fact that the clean, orderly appearance of the instruments opposes the brutal, bloody reality of invasive surgery. The conjunction of minimalism and conceptualism imbues the work with a religious quality, as if everyday objects, once arranged in significant order and displayed on an antiseptic alter, become holy relics infused with the sacrament of a divine power.

Hirst is all about the timeless themes of life, death, faith and beauty, but this is dressed up in the quintessential aesthetic of its time. The way *Still* looks is distinctly 1994 – post-minimalism, post-Jeff Koons' hoovers, post-Modernism, post-Pop, departing from them all but retaining traces of their influence – and could not have been made at any other time in art history. But its subject – the fragility of life, the wish for immortality, faith in medicine – is timeless, expressing the vexations of spirit that inextricably reside at the core of being alive and being human.

This melding of the timeless and the contemporary illustrates the way in which there is always a duality at work in Hirst. Hirst's work hinges on oppositions which conflict with and complement one another. Hirst's work is striking precisely because it flagrantly contradicts itself, forcing the viewer to enter into battle with it and with themselves: *A Thousand Years* (1990), for example, is grotesque and disgusting as the flies feed on the bleeding, rotting cow's head, but the way they flicker in and out of the light, frying in its heat, and the way they breed and live in the face of obliteration is enchanting – here the battle between life and death is laid bare – horrifying and fascinating in equal measure. And the list goes on, as Hirst sets up one contradiction for the viewer to resolve after another: the Spot Paintings are maddeningly simple in form but incomprehensible in their infinity; the Natural History works possess the quiet charm of science at the same time as expressing the horror of death; the Butterfly Paintings are humorous accidents and senseless murders of beauty; and the diamond skull is an act of grotesque ostentation and an heroic victory over death.

The richness of Hirst's art is precisely this tussle between two parts of a duality which he sets up and leaves the viewer to fight out[72]. This duality might be expressed in terms of Nietzsche's Apollo and Dionysus in the sense that it represents a site of conflict between order, on the one hand, and chaos, on the other[73]. There is the Apollonian order of the surgical instruments, bright, pristine, arranged in lines, and the Dionysian chaos of tearing into the living, breathing flesh of life. It is as if Hirst's programme hinges on an Apollonian aesthetic and a Dionysian concept which tends, as all thing in the universe do, towards entropy.

This conflict is endlessly played out in the relationship between the aesthetic of the artwork and its conceptual content, where the way it looks and what it is about are opposed to one another. Hirst's great talent is to ensure that this site of conflict is never jarring, incongruous or clumsy; there is never more aesthetic affectation than is required to express the concept, and there is never more conceptual content than can be read in the aesthetic. In linguistic terms, what he means is transparent in what he says. The conceptual content of *The Physical Impossibility of Death in the Mind of Someone Living* is about fear of death, conveyed in a shark which is big enough to eat you, seemingly swimming towards you in a vat of blue liquid; it makes you think about the fragility of life and the awful contingency of death; the shark instils fear, but its containment and inert lifelessness inspires reassurance, which neatly mirrors the fluctuating relationship we have with the prospect of our own deaths. All these ideas are contained in and manifest by the object before us – shark, glass, water – there is nothing outside of the object that we need to know in

---

[72] Here there is a striking similarity to Martin Creed, who uses a conflict between minimalism and conceptualism to the same end, although, of course, by a very different means. See Chapter VII, Anything and Nothing At All.

[73] See Nietzsche, *The Birth of Tragedy*, § 1-8.

order to understand what the artwork is about. This economy of communication is Hirst's great trick, and is not one to be sniffed at, since we are prone to such despair when art seems obtuse or elitist, difficult to understand or relate to.

Hirst – like all great thinkers – only has one idea, which is refined, reiterated and developed throughout a body of work[74]. This might stink of one trick pony but when you cast your eye over the history of human endeavour, you see that the people who make the most significant, efficacious contributions to thought are specialists whose contribution is deep and narrow, whereas a generalist will be forgotten for casting their net too wide and in too shallow waters. Hirst's one idea is that death is a certainty and a fact, but nonetheless we fear it and we concoct manifold ways – science, medicine, religion, money, art – to delay or deny it. That is everything Hirst is about. It may not be to everyone's taste and some may question the wisdom of the one idea specialist, but great misdeeds have been committed in the name of taste and in pursuit of vapid generalisation. The compelling thing about Hirst is the ingenuity of the manner in which the idea is aesthetically manifest. All his work is iterations of the one idea, but those iterations are discretely different and delicately nuanced.

An artistic practice that consists in the one idea reiterated, explored and extrapolated in different, evolving aesthetic forms is bound to entail repetition. Hirst trades in repetition

---

[74] The use of the word 'idea' here is to be taken broadly. Great thinkers will tend to have a singular notion that they devote their lives to studying and developing, constantly revising and restating it with ever more refinement. Steven Hawking had black holes, Einstein had relativity, AJ Ayer had the verification principle, Rawls had justice as fairness, Nelson Mandela had freedom, and so on. Occasionally, there will be great thinkers who demonstrate incredible depth and breadth of interests, such as Nietzsche, Nozick and Chomsky, but for the most part, insofar as they are academics, a specialism is the norm.

with discrete variation: every Spot Painting repeats the format, but each one has different size spots, different colours and different dimensions; each Natural History work has a different animal, and even the ones that all contain sharks have different sizes and different breeds; the Medicine Cabinets contain different numbers of drugs; and the Kaleidoscope Paintings are different shapes and sizes with an array of different butterflies. The works in a series are superficially similar because they are born of the one stable concept, but, in the language of Nelson Goodman, they are finitely differentiated[75] – the effect they produce differs each time according to the effect of the details. And for Hirst, the devil is in the detail.

This repetition and detail is itself a conceptual gesture in a body of work about death: death repeats itself eternally as long as there is life, unperturbed by the tedium of its repetition; and the only things that render bearable the tedium of the cycle of the human drama are the details of an individual life, which has fleeting moments of elation, tragedy, love and loathing. It is, therefore, part of the meaning of the work that there is something eerily familiar in this grid of spots or that tank of formaldehyde – the sameness of repetition brings home your insignificance in the ghastly cycle of death as just one more speck of dust floating aimlessly into the furnace of the sun; and the differences in aesthetic details echoes the unique beauty of all things, unique in spite of their common end, since, as Jean-Paul Sartre says, 'every existent is born without reason, prolongs itself out of weakness and dies by chance'[76].

---

[75] Nelson Goodman, *Languages of Art*, 2nd edition (Indianapolis: Hackett, 1976), 130-133.

[76] Jean-Paul Sartre, *Nausea*, trans. Robert Baldick (London: Penguin, 1965), 191.

The thing people respond to in Hirst is not, however, this one idea or any of the conceptual content of his work; it is, rather, the aesthetic, which is variously achieved with spectacle, craftsmanship, the sublime or shock and awe. Even the most sceptical, usually ravaged by their own prejudice and ignorance, cannot help but be wowed on occasion by Hirst's aesthetic. There is something about the sight of a highly polished stainless steel cabinet filled with 12,000 hand-crafted pills that only the most sensually impoverished person can resist or deny. Sure, the aesthetic may sometimes have the feel of a lousy trick or a cheap thrill, but the fact that we are nonetheless seduced says more about our base aesthetic sensibilities than it does about Hirst's art.

Once we see Hirst as an aesthetician, it becomes clear why he is so successful; the commercial artworld loathes nothing more than ideas, thinking, intellectuals and rational debate; it despises these things because they can sway – by a well-worded speech and an immaculately argued text – a client away from buying art, whereas the way something looks, its pure aesthetic, unadulterated by rich critical prose, can seduce a client in an instant – and nothing can sway or deny those base aesthetic instincts. Big ideas, indeed, but it is important not to let big money get in the way of big ideas. If you stare deep into the eyes of the sheep in *Away from the Flock* (1994), its cold, watery eyes stare back at you with such grim pleading that you forget about the 90s and all the money, and realise in one crystalline moment of pure sensation that art is the standing possibility of enlightenment through aesthetics, which has absolutely nothing to do with the stacks of money that Damien Hirst has made from his art.

Hirst is in the business of sensations – the yuck of a severed cow's head covered in flies or the wow of a diamond encrusted skull – which is what life is all about. It is those discrete, precious moments when we feel the ground beneath our feet, linger on the touch of a lover's hand and savour the view of the setting sun that define our lives and ultimately have the final word on whether we think it is all worthwhile. Hirst challenges us to recognise that aesthetic engagement is all we can reasonably ask of a cruel world that, from the very moment we are born, has set itself on course to obliterate us.

So how did the value industry blind us to all of this? It was not difficult, nor was it resisted by Hirst. Indeed, he aided and abetted his own fate as he became very wealthy indeed throughout the 90s. Eventually, Hirst became Britain's most expensive living artist, having sold a lot of very expensive art between 2007 and 2008. This gave him the power to do whatever he liked.

In 2007, Hirst's 'Beyond Belief' exhibition reportedly made £130,000,000, while he netted a further £50,000,000 from the sale, to a consortium that included himself and his dealer, Jay Jopling, of the infamous diamond skull, *For the Love of God*. That same year, he superseded Jasper Johns' record for the most expensive work by a living artist sold at auction with *Lullaby, Spring* (2002) for £9,650,000[77]. Then, in 2008, he bypassed his galleries to make £111,000,000 from a vast body of new work at Sotheby's in the sale he called 'Beautiful Inside My Head Forever', on the very night Lehman Brothers filed for Chapter 11 bankruptcy[78].

Hirst is a natural entrepreneur and has always surrounded himself with people, like his celebrated business manager Frank Dunphy, who can realise the optimum potential of his

---

[77] All these figures are reported by Pernilla Holmes, 'The Branding of Damien Hirst', *Art News,* 1 October 2007.
[78] 15 September 2008.

brand. It is said that he negotiates a 75% cut of all sales from his gallerists[79], manages private sales of new works direct from the studio and holds on to, or buys back, old works with the aim of controlling his prices. Somebody with that much business acumen and artistic talent is bound do well, but what he did after becoming the most expensive living artist is nothing short of ludicrous. Genius, but ludicrous.

The diamond skull and the Sotheby's sale drew a line in the sand as the most audacious, impertinent and outrageous things he could do. Hirst could do just about anything and get away with it. So, what did he do next? He did the most surprising thing anyone could imagine: he retired to his garden shed in Devon to confront his final demon – painting, that awkward craft which thwarted him so profoundly that he came up with the idea of the Spot Paintings[80]. After many months in hiding, he emerged with a series of paintings that he had painted himself, with his own hands, without any assistants.

The fruits of these labours were shown, in true Hirst style, at the Wallace Collection, London, which is home to a revered collection of 18th Century French decorative arts, in 2009, in a show called 'No Love Lost': dark, mucky swathes of Prussian Blue, somewhere between still life and Hirst's greatest hits, depicting skulls, cigarettes, roses, lemons, iguanas and shark's jaws. Although almost universally panned by critics as proof that Hirst is a talentless charlatan, this move incomprehensibly enforced the Hirst myth. The paintings were widely thought to be strange and incompetent, but the fact that

---

[79] Also reported by Holmes, 'The Branding of Damien Hirst'.
[80] Hirst has said that he came up with the idea of the Spot Paintings because, as a student at Goldsmiths, he found himself unable to resolve how best to use colour in painting. The frustration, he says, led him to an immaculate grid of spots which looked as if it was painted by a machine, which brought closure to a fraught relationship with painting.

he had the courage and the audacity to do it only cemented his position as the untouchable king of the artworld. Hirst had transcended his own myth by showing terrible paintings at the Wallace Collection and selling them at a premium as *the only artworks he'd ever produced himself*. There were two other exhibitions of paintings, both at White Cube, 'Nothing Matters' (2010) and 'Two Weeks One Summer' (2012), the latter of which inspired Jonathan Jones to compare Hirst to Saif al-Islam Gaddafi[81]. Again, this extreme response only demonstrated that even if Hirst was a delusional despot, he had the courage of a centurion and the impunity of a saint. Strange as it may seem, this was the height of Hirst's powers, since it was only after becoming Britain's most expensive living artist and one of the richest artists in the world that he could make and display his own paintings. Without all that money and fame and notoriety to protect him from what some certainly thought was the hollow truth, it simply would have been impossible, unthinkable.

Hirst can afford to explore with gleeful abandon whatever misadventure takes his fancy because every time a classic Natural History work or a Spot Painting is on the block, the price it achieves guarantees the value of another bizarre painting. This market confidence, bolstered by a gentle shift in artistic direction, accounts for the success of his 2014 'Black Scalpel Cityscapes' series, which met with the warmest critical reception of anything he had done for years. These works were so well-received because whilst they are Hirsty in their shininess and demure brutality, they are also essentially pictures of things, and people are irretrievably drawn to pictures of things above anything else in art.

---

[81] Jonathan Jones, 'Damien Hirst: Two Weeks One Summer – review', *The Guardian,* 22 May 2012.

Hirst had deliberately built up his own mythology to the point where he can get away with anything with the consequence that he will always make money regardless of whether or not he gains any serious critical acclaim. He has successfully manipulated the mechanisms of the value industry to ensure that he generates economic value in everything he does, regardless of anyone's judgement of cultural value. The mythology became so strong, however, that cultural value became so obscured as to be irrelevant. Hirst seemed to be all about the money because that is the one thing that can be relied upon. There is, however, a strange glitch in the story, which explains how the skull, the Sotheby's sale and the paintings created a market confidence that would ultimately privilege economic value over cultural value.

This next part of the story will explain how the value industry made you believe there is nothing more to Hirst than the money. In May 2007, Christie's New York sold *Lullaby, Winter* (2002) for $7,400,000 to an unnamed Asian buyer. So, when *Lullaby, Spring* – the second in a seminal quartet of Pill Cabinets knows as 'The Seasons' – came up for sale at Sotheby's, London, just five weeks later, its record-setting price of £9,600,000 was due in no small part to the confidence generated by the first cabinet, for high prices only beget higher prices. *Lullaby, Winter* was the catalyst that finally drove his market into the stratosphere. The idea that *Lullaby, Winter* has been languishing in some important collection and has been lent out to major retrospectives in London and Doha only gives it kudos, but, in a remarkable twist, the work was never paid for and remained the property of Christie's.

The very event that propelled Hirst was itself an unfulfilled promise. This means that Hirst's meteoric mid-career renaissance as a millionaire and a painter was predicated on an error: although the cabinet realised that price in theory, which begot the price of the next one and so on, the bill was never paid, no money was ever exchanged. In monetary terms, *Lullaby, Winter*, has a null value – it is just a void in Christie's accounts that created an explosion in Hirst's accounts. The high price of the second cabinet, apparently so intimately related to that of the first, was based only on the idea of the price and not the actuality of a transaction having taken place.

The myth of the rich celebrity artist who is more about money than art, then, is sustained by the abiding narrative: the sell-out 'Beyond Belief' show, the diamond skull, the Sotheby's sale and the exhibitions of hand-crafted paintings were, in a sense, made possible by the market confidence generated by the sale of those two Pill Cabinets, rendering Hirst the most expensive living British artist with a licence to do as he wished.

The years 2007 and 2008, for Hirst, were all about the money. Everything about or connected to Hirst that was reported in those years was about vast sums of money being exchanged, and consequently the art – which was, after all, the source of all that money – all but dropped out of the picture. The art was only mentioned as a footnote when an explanation for the origin or cause of the money was needed. The value industry styled Hirst as the miraculous generator of economic value, and with that potent narrative in place it was impossible for a general audience to see the value of the art.

It was not until 2009 that art entered the picture again, with those infamous exhibitions of paintings, 'No Love Lost' and 'Nothing Matters', by which time it was too late to dislodge cultural value from the manacles of economic value. It was, of course, the boom years of 07/08 that motivated Jonathan Jones' scathing attack on Hirst's paintings, accusing him of being so rich and powerful a despot that nobody would dare to discourage him from painting.

But then, from 2009 to 2017, the narrative shifted once again from being about money to being about art. It was as if those paintings, derided as they were, left a bitter taste in the mouths of all whom talked about Hirst's money. Big money for bad art suddenly, as if moral consciousness had been awakened, seemed a difficult idea to stomach for an artworld that backed Hirst's prices so long as the work looked expensive. And therein is the rub – the paintings of 'No Love Lost' did not look like they were, or ever could be, worth £1,000,000 – whereupon the magic of Hirst vanished[82]. It was, to everybody's horror, all about aesthetics all along: it always was and is about the way things look, and these things – wonky, scrawled and blistering with failure – looked like nothing, not even the name of the richest artist in the world, could justify the price tag.

In normal circumstances, an unveiling such as this would cause a career to clamber to a halt and a reputation to come crashing down. But for Hirst, it was an awakening: if it is all about the way art looks and not about how much it costs, then what else is possible? For Hirst's supporters and detractors alike, the whole debacle proved he was immune to failure. So, given that Hirst could not fail and given that he would reap millions no matter what, and given that it made no material difference to the price when the art looked bad, the narrative shifted, almost over night. Economic value, which had been so newsworthy, if not interesting, stepped into the shadows,

---

[82] The authentic, hand-painted Hirsts range in price from £500,000 for a very tiny picture to around £3,000,000 for quite a large one. This scale is about average for fresh-from-the-studio new works, so there was nothing in particular about these paintings that changed the substance of Hirst's pricing.

leaving cultural value to have its time in the spotlight. After all, once the richest artist had made the worst art, it was incumbent on every level-headed critic to think seriously about what in his body of work was, in fact, good for culture, and it turned out that favourable conclusions could be reached without mammoth effort.

This was partly because secondary market prices had levelled and, in some cases, stagnated or even dropped, so there was nothing newsworthy to report, and partly because during the period between 2009 and 2017 Hirst genuinely returned to form, making some of his best work since the early 90s. However, that claim must be tempered: 'best work' here indicates that it was better than anything he had produced for years precisely because during this period he introduced new concepts and series, so it was refreshing and significant, but still only half as good as anything he made in the 90s. The very fact that we are inclined to have a discussion about whether this period produced the 'best work' since the 90s is indicative of the shift in emphasis – Hirst was marking art which it was possible to speak of in art critical, rather than purely monetary, terms.

The period 2009 to 2017 can be seen as an attempt by Hirst and his People to promote the notion that Hirst is, after all that money, a serious artist. During this time, there were two major retrospectives – in London (Tate Modern, 2012) and Doha (Qatar Museums Authority, 2013) – which did a great deal to fix the narrative more firmly on the art, both of them being respectable, scholarly and well-curated surveys of a career. Gagosian, in 2012, staged a bizarre world-wide exhibition, 'The Complete Spot Paintings 1986-2011', which was intended as an academic survey of the Spot Paintings to demonstrate their variation and subtlety. Then there were exhibitions of new work 'Entomology Cabinets and Paintings' (White Cube, Hong Kong, 2013), Scalpel Blade Paintings (White Cube, Sao Paulo, 2014), culminating in the epic 'Treasures from the Wreck of the Unbelievable' (Pinault Collection, Venice, 2017). All of this was marketed as art with little mention of money, focusing on art-friendly notions such as 'change of direction' or 'consolidation of ideas'.

'Treasures from the Wreck of the Unbelievable' was a heroic return to form. It hinged on the old tropes of aesthetic spectacle and conceit, but this time on an unprecedented grand scale. It was vast, spread over two museums and containing 189 pieces, with works on every scale from the miniscule to the gigantic. A veritable spectacle in every dimension. The artefacts, so the narrative goes, belonged to a former slave, Cif Amotan II, who lived in the 1st and 2nd Centuries CE. They were found by archaeologists at the bottom of the ocean, off the coast of East Africa, in the wreck of a ship called The Unbelievable. Hirst took charge of the excavations and spent 10 years curating a museum exhibition of the findings. For each of the 189 pieces, there are three editions, each with its own aesthetic – one excavated from the seabed encrusted with coral, one museum copy in plaster and one perfectly restored to its former glory – and two artist proofs, totalling 2835 works.

It takes mammoth self-belief, faithful gallerists, unwavering confidence in your market and unimaginable gal to stage a show of such magnitude. But Hirst presented it, against all odds, as an aesthetic spectacle that hailed a return to the glory days. The spectacle was quintessentially Hirst, and the conceit was so deep and immaculately executed that it was almost believable. The grandiose statue of Hirst holding hands with Micky Mouse was one of the giveaways, but almost everything else was designed to perpetuate and enforce the narrative, with no corners cut and no expense spared.

Glass cabinets, under spotlights in darkened rooms, contained coins, pots and weapons, as if culled from an archaeological site; crumbling, decrepit sculptures displayed alongside 'museum copies'; statues covered in corals and barnacles from languishing for two thousand years on the seabed; backlit photographs of divers rescuing from the ocean floor the very items you now behold; gold, so much gold, and diamonds and jewels plundered from the wreckage of an ancient ship; a scale model, reimagining the ship and how it carried its loot; and each and every item catalogued and contextualised with a museum-style wall-text. It was an epic, breathless experience of nearly religious proportions, where no acquaintance with the facts – of the $60,000,000 it cost to make, the $1,000,000,000 it could sell for – even faintly dents the sheer awe and wonderment[83]. This, at last, was the Hirst that we remember and love: the artist who would and could go to the trouble and expense of dumping his sculptures in the ocean, so their 'discovery' by divers could be photographed and documented; who would then make a documentary about it, and insist to the world it is genuine archaeology, rather than admit it is multi-million-pound contemporary art that he made just because he could.

Hirst will always divide opinion, but it is important that we see how the myth was, in the final analysis, all about money and nothing whatsoever to do with art. And it is that myth, so

[83] The figure, $60,000,000, was suggested to me by somebody I met in Venice at the time. Other reports I have heard put it at $66,000,000. Kenny Schacter says between £50,000,000 and £100,000,000, as well as suggesting the $1,000,000,000 sales figure. It hardly matters. It cost a lot of money. See Kenny Schacter, 'Is This Show Worth a Billion Dollars? A Few Thoughts on Damien Hirst's New Venture in Venice', *artnet*, 24 April 2017.

gleefully weaved by the value industry, that forms popular opinion of Hirst. Beneath all that, however, there is, as we have now seen, some important and culturally valuable art that history will not forget. As much as can be said and written, the final proof of Hirst's artistic merit is in the lived experience of the work itself. It only really makes sense if you look, with an open mind, upon those 9000 pills in *Lullaby, Spring* with the wistful hope of salvation in medicine and only see in the pristine surface of the cabinet the reflection of your mortal face, forever decaying as the rich get richer and the poor get poorer.

The Pay Me Girl Has Had Enough of the Bleeps

Hirst's trajectory from making some great art early on to becoming more famous for the money than for the art, and then gradually reversing the balance between money and art reflects how the artworld, at least in the UK, went full circle. Money, in the decade since the Great Crash of 2008, became less prominent in the artworld discourse, probably because nobody has any and because those who have it should feel embarrassed for flaunting it in a time of crisis. The shift of focus from money to art is best evidenced by the decline of the YBAs, who have been side-lined for more artistically vital, more culturally and socially relevant artists. The British artworld, at least, began to search for something else... particularly focusing on art which is about identity politics or grassroots political issues, all of which happened concurrently with the global financial crisis, which is undoubtedly not a coincidence. The YBAs who helped to construct the contemporary British artworld also signalled its change of direction, but this time they did so by their conspicuous demise.

Back in the 1990s, while Britpop luvvie, Blur bassist Alex James, was busy spending £1,000,000 on cocaine and champagne[84], the YBAs got extremely rich from selling shocking new art to an insatiable art market which advanced well into the 21st century. The unspeakable euphoria fuelled ever more excess and ever more art, bolstered by toxic debt and the New Labour mantra 'things can only get better'. The great art bubble continued to inflate and to float ever higher until one day the force that propelled it just vanished, an event that was later solidified by the Great Crash. But there was one event that started the ball rolling by finally ending the heyday of the YBAs.

It all came crashing down when Hirst covered a platinum cast of a human skull in 8601 diamonds and sold it for £50,000,000. Everyone gasped and cringed as BBC *Newsnight* presenter Kirsty Wark asked him if he thought there was anything obscene about that. Hirst bit his lip and the tumble weed tumbled. 'Hopefully', he said, 'it's not about money'. But of course, as he would later admit in an interview with the then White Cube Director of Exhibitions, Tim Marlow, it *was* all about money; it was about how much money you could throw at death. But it was also, we swiftly surmised, about how much money you could throw at art before you killed it.

And that is how it ended: the most hopelessly ostentatious artwork became the most expensive piece ever sold by a living artist, and there was no longer anything more the YBAs could do to shock, sensationalise or scandalise. That diamond skull was the last and highest parting with the 90s and Cool Britannia. The political death of that New Labour era of

---

[84] Alex James, *Bit of a Blur* (London: Abacus, 2008), 228.

hope and renewal occurred somewhat earlier, in 2003, with the ill-advised invasion of Iraq. Art hung on a bit longer before it finally gave up.

Despite the death of the YBA era, its zombies still walk the Earth with varying degrees of success. Some of the artists, like Marcus Harvey and Mat Collishaw have continued respectable careers by fading quietly into the background, while others, like Gary Hume and Marc Quinn, linger in the middle-distance with an unfathomable faith in their winning formula. Michael Landy and Chris Ofili continue to surprise with nuanced changes of direction, while Jenny Saville and Fiona Rae are quietly, consistently good. Sam Taylor-Johnson found a new career as a film director and the art she makes now is a far cry from that of her youth. Even Emin matured somewhat in style and form, if not in content, proving that it was time to grow up. Occasionally one of them pops up as if nothing has changed, such as when Jake and Dinos Chapman wheeled out another round of Hitler watercolours at a show in the sleepy English seaside town of Hastings in 2014. The paradox is that it is difficult not to feel a tinge of delight in front of a carefully doctored Hitler watercolour, but as the aesthetic high fades a curious sort of 90s hangover begins to set in. One of Hirst's saving graces is that in every show since 2008 he has produced something new, rather than rehashed the old, and the same is true for Emin, which is why they stand above their peers as the most enduring artists of the movement.

When groups of artists who were inextricably tied to a milieu continue to do the same things in a world which is so different from when they started, it looks archaic and awkward. This was typified by Sarah Lucas' British Pavilion at the 2015 Venice Biennale: as Sarah Lucas work, it was great, but as art to represent Britain on the international stage it looked tired, as if we are eternally stuck in the 90s. As we watched Lucas beam with pride in the front of the world's press, it was difficult to blame her for just doing her shtick, but it was misguided of the British Council to allow the world this antiquated view of British art.

Meanwhile, Hirst was building a mausoleum to the excesses of his glory days – a museum in Vauxhall to house his art collection, bought with all the gold he did not splurge in the Groucho Club. And then there is Charles Saatchi, whose influence began to erode as he started selling off his YBA treasures: he was forced, as a result of a protracted dispute, to sell his Hirst's back to Hirst himself, and then he sold his seminal Emins. As we have seen, nothing he could buy after that would reassert his power as chief tastemaker, save a few Christian Rosas. One of the surest signs of the end of days was the quiet plateau reached by Hirst's prices. The sale of Hirst's *Lullaby, Winter* for a paltry £3,000,000 in 2015 was a grim reminder of the fact that back in the day it would have fetched £5-7,000,000 in a heartbeat. It was time to move on.

The glory days are gone, and any attempt, sincerely nostalgic or otherwise, to recapture them is foolhardy. The narrative of the YBAs was, in the final analysis, always a narrative about money, unthinkable economic value that injected a starving market, a stagnating nation, with mystical powers of influence and wealth. But money comes and goes. The thing that remains, and will do so for ever, is the art, and as the narrative of money subsides, the cultural value of those artists and their work becomes apparent. The YBAs created works which changed the face of British art and will adorn the museums of the future and fill the history books. Economics is transient, whereas culture is eternal, which is something the value industry – so hellbent on money and myth – cannot deny.

VI. Weapons of Massive Consumption

Why celebrity does not add instant value

It is one thing for artists and collectors to create myths that embellish and contextualise their work, which are then co-opted by the market to humanise the process of economic exchange, but it is quite another thing for the value-adding myths to be created by someone else. Sometimes myths are created by the market to justify prices, or by critics and historians who wish to immortalise the art and artists in their immediate favour, and sometimes myths just emerge as so much hearsay through the mechanisms of the mass media. In all such cases, the myths still add value, but, contrary to the cases thus far considered, that value is decisively intended to be either cultural or economic because the mythmaker will have an agenda. Here we shall consider how the myth of celebrity is used to attempt to add value to very poor simulations of art, and we shall use these celebrity artists to arrive at a definition of the artworld. For the YBAs, celebrity and economic value followed one another like day and night, but that was because their work possessed inherent cultural value. That is, the entailment relationship between celebrity status and high prices was not an accident or affectation; it was driven, as we saw, by the inherent value of the work being produced. Now, however, we shall see cases where the work possesses diminishing cultural value and minimal economic value, and there is nothing celebrity status can do to change that.

Don't Break My Art, My Achy Breaky Art

Miley Cyrus once said her goal in life is 'to not die a pop pop dumb dumb'[85]. She was searching for redemption from a life lived in the spotlight: haunted by the ghost of Hannah Montana, plagued by a string of pop hits, cursed with a famous father and stupendous wealth, all played out through a haze of sex and drugs. So Cyrus turned to art in an attempt to save her soul.

Cyrus had a difficult time in 2014. She spent a stint in hospital and her dog died, not to mention the gruelling schedule of her Bangerz tour. In the midst of all the chaos, she took time out to reflect on the tumultuous events of her life and on her posterity, and concluded that she would 'freak out' if she died having only ever been a trailblazing popstar. This introspection gave rise to Cyrus' big break into the artworld, with her debut exhibition, 'Dirty Hippie' at the offices of *V Magazine,* New York City.

Cyrus makes exactly the sort of art you'd expect: garish, clumsy, cheap, poppy sculptures that could only be the result of petulant, spoiled indulgence; collages of found objects, including vibrators, teddy bears, beads, hamster toys, party hats

---

[85] Miley Cyrus quoted in Kevin Mcgarry, 'Miley Cyrus Presents', *V Magazine*, 29 August 2014. All quotes are from this source.

and drug paraphernalia. These conglomerations of sickly-sweet coloured plastic objects are reminiscent of Mike Kelley, on a somewhat charitable interpretation. Pristinely glued together to form phallic symbols, headdresses set upon pure white mannequin heads and bees-nest bundles of assorted detritus on plinths, they tread a line between abstraction and figuration, expressing a frustration with the shallowness of consumer culture, as if they were the fruits of an infant Jeff Koons' untutored loins.

The story behind these sculptures is a gripping tale. The raw materials were donated by adoring fans or otherwise collected on tour by a popstar desperate to relieve herself of her abundant fortune. This accumulation of stuff inspired Cyrus to think about how money does not buy happiness. She reflected on her charmed existence: despite the trappings of fame, she concluded that material possessions and adoration do nothing to cure the existential boredom she routinely dulls by smoking weed every day. Cyrus then started making art out of this clutter in order to both express her discontent with that clutter and in an attempt to create something more transcendent and durable than her pop career. It is a familiar story, straight out of Nietzsche, via Sophocles: the birth of art out of the spirit of discontent with consumerism and popular culture.

Cyrus follows in an illustrious line, where comparisons could be drawn with the likes of Koons, Hirst and Richard Phillips. Like Phillips, she exposes the emptiness beneath the sheen of celebrity; like Hirst, she uses a disparity between the materials and the ideas to raise questions about value; and like Koons, the sheer banality of it all is overblown to the point of irresistibility. Furthermore, the art of Miley Cyrus possesses the charming duality of an outward-looking critique of culture and an intimate expression of her tormented inner self.

Cyrus' own explanation of her art sums it up perfectly: 'They say money can't buy happiness and it's totally true...Money can buy you a bunch of shit to glue to a bunch of other shit that will make you happy, but...obviously the shit you buy doesn't make you happier because I'm sitting here gluing a bunch of junk to stuff'. At the grand old age of 21, she was in the grip of an existential crisis, which, she believed, art was a perfectly logical response to.

The artworks that this crisis brought forth certainly look like art: collaged sculptures, a fusion of the contemporary trend for upcycling found or appropriated materials with the traditional craft of sculpting. And they are expressive, in the manner of RG Collingwood's injunction that art should arouse in its audience an emotional response to the artist's state of mind as embodied in the work[86]. Moreover, they also comment more broadly on the human condition in the grip of late capitalism. But, at the time, there was something awry in the claim, implicit in all the write-ups, that this art should have value as art, namely cultural value, precisely because it was made by a celebrity. The idea was that Cyrus' celebrity status infused the work with artistic kudos because she was expressing herself in sculpture, as she does in her music, thus demonstrating creative versatility.

There is an inherent perversion in the public response to contemporary art: when an established artist presents a work that mildly offends out-dated sensibilities about what art is, there is an outrage which asks, 'Is it art?'; but when a celebrity, well-accomplished in some field of entertainment but with little artistic background, presents a work that minimally

---

[86] RG Collingwood, *The Principles of Art.*

simulates the appearance of art, nobody bats an eyelid. When a high-profile event like the Turner Prize proffers Emin's *My Bed* or Martin Creed's *Work No. 227 The lights going on and off* (2001), a braying public demands blood, but when a self-indulgent celebrity with too much time on their hands convinces a gallery to show their artistic fumblings, such as Miley Cyrus' sculptures or Pete Docherty's well-meant but ghastly blood letters, the public accepts it as both art and another glittering example of that celebrity's genius. There is something very wrong indeed here, and it is not even theoretical – this is how people actually respond to art in a routine and unthinking way. The catastrophe here is both profound and ordinary.

The question of how to respond to Cyrus' work, then, is vexed by the willingness to accept celebrity art while rejecting genuine artworks. A fair, intellectually responsible judgement requires that we divorce the work from the person who created it, as if applying an aesthetic version of John Rawls' Veil of Ignorance whereby all judgements are to be made without the slightest knowledge of your or anyone else's position in the grand scheme of things so that everything is treated fairly[87]. On this view, Cyrus' art looks like that kind of trendy, disposable commercial art that ticks all the right boxes to buy today and sell tomorrow. It is impossible to deny that Miley Cyrus has made a decent *simulation* of art, the illusion of which is sustained by unfathomable self-belief. Nonetheless, if you want edifying contemporary art which does more than just look like art, then you could do better than the idling of a drugged-up, bored, pop pop dumb dumb.

For the value industry, celebrity status is enough to guarantee economic value, since somebody will buy the work,

---

[87] John Rawls, *A Theory of Justice*, revised edition (Cambridge: Harvard University Press, 1999), 118.

no matter how good it is, *because* it is by Miley Cyrus. This, given what we have already said about the power of operative mythologies to create value, cannot be contested. The point of contention, however, arises when we consider the further claim, implicit in the judgement of economic value and the optimistic comparisons with Kelley and Koons, is that the work possesses some *cultural value.* To be sure, some of that cultural value derives from the work's being sufficiently comparable to other extant sculpture, but some of it – more than an insignificant proportion, to be sure – arises from Cyrus' celebrity status. Its cultural value, if it has any, derives from the novelty of Cyrus expressing herself, and thus showcasing her talents, in a different artistic medium.

The idea is that Cyrus is already an artist, a music artist, who makes a living from the expression of human feeling in significant aesthetic form, so when she transfers that skillset from music to sculpture, nothing is, artistically speaking, lost or changed. It is exactly the power of celebrity that makes this transference possible: in virtue of being internationally adored, lucrative and famous, she can switch at will from one artform to another, making no difference to the integrity of her message or aesthetic programme and effortlessly imbuing sculpture, as much as music, with the magic of her touch. Although the myth of celebrity is powerful, it is not powerful enough to transfigure *anything* into art. To understand why this is, we need to think soberly about what art really is and how cultural value cannot simply be magicked out of nowhere in the same way that economic value can be.

More Snoop Dogg than Snoop Doig

We shall now consider a similar case to further illustrate the failure of celebrity to create cultural value. The key difference here, which will make the point about value easier to digest, is that the art in question is bad by any standard.

Inspired by the pattern on a cushion, Snoop Dogg, while staying at the Palazzo Versace hotel, Venice, once made a painting that sold on eBay for $10,200. The stroke of genius came when Swedish sock giants, Happy Socks, commissioned Snoop to design a range based on his abstract paintings. The promotional video, hopefully now lost in the depths of the internet, shows a half-naked Snoop, stoned and surrounded by female assistants, making light work of a number of canvases. It is one of the great insights into a master painter's mysterious creative process, on a par with Hans Namuth's film of Jackson Pollock. It shows Snoop intoxicated with the Dionysian spirit, bringing Apollonian order to his convoluted emotions: great, fevered gestures of wild abandon that, in the luminous glow of the studio, produce monumental, affecting works of art.

The paintings trace the way the hand struggles to express, in purely visual terms, the yearnings of the soul. Snoop explains the visceral immediacy of his work: 'sometimes the music in my life don't explain exactly what I'm going through, so [painting] is another piece of the puzzle'[88]. Snoop could have done anything to fill this gaping hole in his life, but he turned to the hallowed art of painting. It is Miley Cyrus all over again. But there is a difference – Snoop's paintings are bad, extraordinarily, exceptionally bad by any imaginable standard, whereas Cyrus' sculptures are, at worst, passable. The quality, however, makes no difference – these celebrities are celebrated and valorised for their aesthetic prowess. Art, it seems, is the

---

[88] Quoted in Danna Takako, 'Catch a Glimpse of Snoop Dogg, the Artist, in Action', *Dazed and Confused*, 28 October 2014.

next best refuge for beleaguered celebrities, after Scientology and cocaine.

The expectation is that Snoop's celebrity, and his own operative mythology, will add value to the paintings. To be sure, it is expected that this will be cultural value in the same way as it was with Cyrus: the paintings will be seen as another string to Snoop's indefinitely complex bow, wherein he is expressing himself in painting as in music, demonstrating artistic prowess and versatility of spirit that lends his painting a special kudos all of its own. It seems that the very act of making art affords a catharsis which the likes of Snoop and Cyrus cannot find elsewhere. You only have to look at the calm on Snoop's face as he attacks the canvas to see that painting has relieved him of a pain that would otherwise have no outlet. Art, as we know, saves lives – imagine what would have happened to the young hooligan from Leeds if a wayward fly had not incongruously landed itself on a freshly primed canvas.

The problem is that no amount of celebrity mythology can imbue the work with a cultural value akin to art, no matter how much economic value can be extracted from the nature of celebrity. Snoop's paintings are aesthetically inept, uninteresting, ugly, unstimulating and pointless, and as such possess little, if any, cultural value at all. Any and all economic value – all $10,200 – of that first painting derived from Snoop's celebrity status, as did the subsequent offer of collaboration from Happy Socks. After all, who cares what imbecilic pattern, scrawled into being by a stoned fool, exists on one's socks – half of which is within shoes, the other half of which is obscured by trousers. That offer of collaboration was an economic decision based on celebrity kudos and had absolutely nothing to do with aesthetics. The problem is this:

the cultural value of Snoop's and Cyrus' work derives from the nature of celebrity and not from the nature of art, so their works may be valuable as celebrity relics but not as art and certainly not as art with any significant cultural value in the sense that we have been discussing. One thing is for certain: it is not just about the fact that one celebrity makes terrible art and the other makes almost acceptable art – it is, for once, deeper than aesthetics. It is do with the fact that neither possess cultural value and one final example will demonstrate what it means for a thing to have cultural value as art.

Franco, My Dear, I Don't Give a Damn

James Franco is an actor, writer, musician, English Literature graduate, teacher, director and celebrity. But he is also an artist in a way that Snoop and Cyrus never could be. His art takes as its subject the heart-breaking sycophancy and emptiness of the artworld itself. It is rich in a cultural value that does not entirely derive from his celebrity status; indeed, he does not need his celebrity to do much of the work for him because that which he is producing is always already art. Celebrity here adds tangential economic value, whereas in the cases we have just seen, it was supposed to add cultural value as well.

Franco is entrancing on screen: whether he is waving a shotgun and screaming 'look at my shit' in *Spring Breakers* or playing the apocalypse party host as a goofy version of himself in *This is the End*, he exudes the kind of magnetism that Hollywood dreams of but rarely gets. Perhaps what is less well-publicised is that Franco is a gifted writer, following in the tradition of Bret Easton Ellis. *Bungalow 89* is a short story that thinly fictionalises Franco's life in Hollywood[89] – wafers of fiction that scarcely gloss over reality and in fact cut too deep for comfort is a trademark of Franco's practice – always playing one uneasy step from reality. The story finds Franco residing on Sunset Boulevard, reminiscing about the first time he met Gus van Sant whom he treats like a father figure but on whom he also, obviously, has some kind of crush, an unresolved sexual desire that keeps their relationship warm but ambivalent. Central to the plot is Franco's refusal to sleep with Lindsey Lohan; instead he reads her JD Salinger stories which uncomfortably mirror her disastrous relationship with her own mother. It is a slick, compelling tale of manipulation, confused sexual energy and the sheer boredom of super-stardom, aptly illustrated by the infinitely glossy paintings of Richard Phillips.

It is, like everything Franco does, self-conscious pastiche, faltering somewhere between critique and worship, that simultaneously exposes the heart and conceals the surface. Franco puts maximum energy and devotion into everything he does, but you can never quite tell whether he is doing that sincerely or if he is just playing the game. Franco's standard operating procedure is to play it just that bit more than anybody else would dare: in *Spring Breakers*, he is a bit too joyful in being unhinged, in *Bungalow 89* he is too explicit about his primarily sexual attraction to Gus van Sant, and in *King Cobra* he is eerily collected beneath the surface. Moreover, he is not content with being an actor, even a great and successful actor, so he is a director as well, studies literature in his spare time and tries his hand at music, teaching and politics. Franco is always too much, goes too far and pushes it over the edge. And if you push it all the way every time like that, nobody says a thing; indeed, the world thinks you are a genius because

---

[89] James Franco, 'Bungalow 89', *Vice*, 10 June 2014.

every time you are always that one unthinkable step ahead of everyone else.

Franco is able to do this because he and Hollywood have a reciprocal relationship: Hollywood feeds off his looks, talent and press attention, claiming the credit for the construction and maintenance of another star; and Franco uses that status to perpetuate his own myth as the spectacular polymath and thus enforces the Hollywood dream that stars make money and money makes stars. Franco is a movie star in the classic mould, embodying the ideals and realities of Hollywood effortlessly and with such finesse that it looks as if he can do no wrong. It is as if he is the subject of a Heideggarian creation myth, whereby he had emerged from the very rocks of the Hills and was Thrown into the Canyons, alone and burdened with the task of finding the path to the limelight of his destiny.

Art is just one of the areas in which Franco chooses to spend his hard-earned commercial cache. One of Franco's exhibitions, 'Fat Squirrel', at Siegfried Contemporary, London (2015), presented paintings and collages depicting a surprising combination of overweight animals and narcissistic self-portraits. Before that, he staged 'New Film Stills' (Pace New York, 2014), in which he used his own pretty face to rework Cindy Sherman's celebrated Film Stills series; and 'Psycho Nacirema' (Pace London, 2013), with YBA Douglas Gordon, who is famed for his work, *24 Hour Psycho* (1993), in which he slowed down Hitchcock's film to two frames per second so that it runs for twenty-four hours.

There is something captivating about Franco's art, which is the same thing that is always captivating about Franco. Walking around 'Psycho Nacirema', for instance, you had that same awkward feeling of immersion and repulsion as you do for his character in *Spring Breakers* – the delirious push-pull of seduction that he always enacts on and off screen. But his art is flawed in a way that nothing else he does is: there is something desperate and poorly executed (despite having behind it the right thought process) in the slapdash rendition of the Bates Motel, the lazy Sherman remake and the puerile comedy of fat squirrels. 'Fat Squirrel', in particular, was grippingly self-indulgent: portraits of himself as James Dean, suggesting an affinity; portly deer engaged in a threesome, perverting a Disney classic; obese squirrels, dogs and horses that seem snatched from BuzzFeed; and a portrait of Gus van Sant looking, as you would expect by now, rugged and strong and desirable. Franco did not, of course, paint the pictures himself, which is a sign that he is doing commercial art properly; he had a 'pet painter' to do them for him, creating kitsch, watery illustrations on which he scrawled the titles in the same manic script he used on the walls of his Bates Motel.

It is, when you look at it carefully, not about fat animals or film stars at all; it is about Franco getting away with it. It is as if he felt caught between his conflicting identities as Hollywood star and aspiring intellectual, always swaying towards the latter because he, like anyone with half a brain, does not want to die a pop pop dumb dumb.

The case of Franco, however, differs markedly from Cyrus or Snoop, no matter how similar it may seem at first glance. The primary similarity, in the first instance, resides in the fact of a celebrity making slapdash art because they can get away with it, aided and abetted by the institutions of the artworld. The difference, and it is significant, is that Franco knows what he is doing: he has a conscious, educated sense of art history and theory which entails that he is making art within the parameters of both the discourse of contemporary art, which includes intertextual reference to and appropriation of art itself, and the trappings and limitations of the commercial artworld. The Sherman, Hitchcock and Gordon pieces might be utterly banal, but they qualify as art in a way that Cyrus' dumb sculptures and Snoop's horrible paintings never could achieve. Granted, he does not make very good art, but for once that is not the point. Franco does not need to make good art because he is doing something infinitely more important. He is making legitimate, historically and theoretically entrenched art that has interesting ideas at its heart and an accessible, but superficially edgy, aesthetic on its surface.

Aside from successfully selling bad art to rich people, Franco is using his art to expose a chasm in the heart of the artworld, which is ordinarily glossed over by the illusion that famous artists are artists before they are celebrities. His art has an unsubtle, clumsy critique of the artworld as its subject and a cheap simulation of lucrative artistic styles as its aesthetic. That Bates Motel stage set and those messy paintings of obese animals are tongue-in-cheek simulations of contemporary art designed to mock the kinds of things that pass for art in the commercial artworld. Franco is making commercially viable art about the artworld whose actual quality pales in comparison to its basic legitimacy as blue-chip art. The commercial artworld does not care if the work is good so much as it cares if it is the right kind of product, so Franco's coup succeeds in virtue of the fact that the art is indistinguishable from the all the other stuff that sells.

The trick, for Franco, is that self-awareness – and a megagallery like Pace will lap it up as if it is starved of milk and honey. The fact that these massive commercial galleries will do anything – even exhibit James Franco – to get their hands on the coolest cultural capital reveals their profound disrespect – even contempt – for the cultural value of art. Anybody who sincerely cares about art as a cultural product would draw the line somewhere; and somebody who represents the estates of Rothko, Picasso, de Kooning and Judd would surely draw the line long before Franco. If you scratch the surface of the artworld, underneath you find a market so wanton that it will betray culture for glory. So when the perfect Hollywood star, adept in everything he attempts, appears with some art, Pace cannot resist because this perfect celebrity has made something that looks and feels just like the art that Pace sells. But everyone is so intoxicated that nobody discerns the kinks in the armour: Franco, like Nietzsche, is touching art with a hammer as with a tuning fork to hear the hollow sound of bloated entrails.

Franco's work has cultural value because it seeks meaning in something outside of celebrity and Franco's internal life; it seeks meaning in a critique of the artworld. Franco's celebrity only adds economic value, but the work is – independently of his celebrity – already art of a certain historically situated and commercially viable kind. It is art made by a celebrity that is worth slightly more because it is made by a celebrity who is especially multi-talented. Celebrity was, of course, the thing that opened the doors of Pace to Franco in the first place, but that does not entail that celebrity is part of the cultural value of his art. Rather, the cult of personality here adds value to stuff that is already art, but celebrity is still not very efficacious in creating value independently of some inherent value in the things themselves, which is what Snoop and Cyrus are hoping for. They think their work is meaningful because it expresses their feelings and the world thinks it is valuable because they are celebrities, but Franco is looking through the lens of art history and theory, which makes all the difference.

It is obscene to say that art is a subjective concept such that if Snoop thinks he is making art then he is, since this does nothing to distinguish art from anything else, which contradicts the fact that we think of art as somehow distinct. Moreover, the fact that we can scarcely agree on a definition of art does not prove there is not one. The distinctness of art is not found in the peculiar qualities of the things we call artworks, but nor is it in the arbitrary subjectivity of a given observer. It is located in a network of practices that Snoop and Cyrus stand outside of.

There is a sense in which we tacitly agree on a fluid but operationally sufficient definition of art that has its philosophical origins in Arthur Danto and George Dickie[90]. Dickie's version, known as the Institutional Theory, is often ignored because it throws up some curious philosophical problems, but at its core it is fundamentally correct about the nature of the artworld[91]. This is the view that 'art' is that which is produced within the artworld, which consists of artists, critics, gallerists, curators, museums, the market, art schools and the audience. If you are reading this, then you are probably in the artworld, too. The institutions of the artworld are engaged in the legitimation of cultural products which, through discourse, determine the boundaries of art from the inside.

In simple terms, this means that the artworld itself decides what is and what is not art, and it does this by discerning how an artefact relates to the history and theory of previously existing art. For example, Cyrus' sculptures do not

---

[90] See Danto, 'The Artworld', and Dickie, *Art and the Aesthetic*.
[91] A good summary of both Danto's and Dickie's theories and some of their main problems can be found in Massimiliano Lacertosa, 'The Artworld and the Institutional Theory of Art: An Analytic Confrontation', *The SOAS Journal of Postgraduate Research*, vol. 8 (2015).

qualify as art if somebody from outside of the artworld says they are good or interesting or even profound, but they do qualify as art if a somebody within the artworld says, for example, that they look like Mike Kelley and are conceptually reminiscent of Jeff Koons. Qualification as art depends upon the right discourse from the right people. Although this seems elitist and flies in the face of a pretheoretical notion that art is a wholly subjective concept in every dimension, it is not too dissimilar from everything else in human culture. In fashion, it is not enough to make clothes which are adored by your friends who have no connection to the fashion industry – you are not practicing fashion, as such, you are only making clothes. Similarly, we may well all cook, and therefore consider ourselves to be cooks of some quality or another, but we are not all chefs, for to be a chef requires a degree of legitimation from a network of professionals. The same, to varying degrees, applies to football, singing and driving, and many other things besides. Even though the boundaries between a cook and chef, or a painter and an artist, may be fluid, that does not mean there are no such boundaries – all such distinctions are governed by the operative discourse of a network of professionals whereby you are either on the inside or outside. It is, unfashionable as it may be to say so, a binary concept.

In Danto's version, which is concerned less with the people and practices of the artworld and more focused on ideas, art is differentiated from mere things by the fact that it possesses an atmosphere of history and theory, such that an artefact is art insofar as it is historically and/or theoretically related to previous artefacts of art. This means that art can be perceptually indiscernible from mere things but is distinguished by the ideas it embodies. On this view, history and theory are the lens through which things are made and looked at, which is what makes them art; often people cannot see art when they encounter it because they are not looking through the lens of the artwork. It is clear, then, that this is the source of our confidence in the claim that Franco is making art with an eye through the lens of history and theory, for the artefacts he makes are clearly – rather too clumsily, in fact – related to and derived from previous episodes in the history of art. As a matter of fact, Danto's theory describes the way things are in reality: it allows that whilst anything *can be* a work of art, not everything *is*, since the presence or absence of history and theory makes the distinction in practice. After all, hardly anyone – whether inside or outside the artworld – wants *everything* to be art.

It is another matter entirely whether history and theory are properties that inhere in the artwork, there to be perceived by any sufficiently trained observer, or whether they are imputed to the work by discourse within the exclusive structure of the artworld. However, it cannot thereby be denied that history and theory are the essential arbiters of what is and what is not art. Furthermore, there is nothing in this that requires everybody to be an expert: a smattering of historical and theoretical knowledge can enable a casual observer to discern art where it is present, just as a moderately competent taster can discern whether a sauce is hollandaise or béarnaise.

It is often thought that Danto and Dickie present mutually exclusive theories and that Danto's is an improvement upon Dickie's, but a theory of value could use both. Cultural value is due, in part, to an artefact possessing the history and theory of art, for it is that which makes it valuable to culture. Indeed, the only way we can know the cultural value of an artwork is to compare it to other similar works in the history of art and to extant theories by way of explanation. Conversely, economic value depends upon the notion that the artworld, like all clubs, is something you have to be on the inside of in order to understand its products and practices. The price of art only makes sense if you are acquainted with the conventions of pricing, which depends upon your being within the artworld in some capacity. For example, it is only from being inside the artworld that the pricing of artworks according to size and artist makes sense: generally speaking, a Hirst is a Hirst and the bigger they get, the more expensive they are, regardless of whether it is a painting, cabinet, sculpture or formaldehyde work; whereas Bacons are priced according to a judgement of scarcity, so that a rare pope is worth more than a common pope, regardless of the size of either. This pricing system does the same for the work's quality and age, and the vivacity of the artist's brand, which only really makes any sense at all if you already more or less know how the artworld operates. So whilst the price of art seems arbitrary, you get the hang of it organically enough with practice and exposure.

It is interesting to consider how, in the most general terms, one might hold both Danto's and Dickie's theories simultaneously, since, apart from the theory of value here presented, they both furnish an aesthetician with different parts of the puzzle. However, that is not our project here. If we are pushed to choose, we should do well to settle with Danto, since he best responds to the conundrum of why mere celebrity status does not add value.

It is precisely because Dickie's approach allows that someone from within the artworld only has to compare Cyrus' work to Kelley's and Snoop's to Pollock's to give it the status of art that we must here reject it. If we were to concede this then the value of art would simply be a function of the say-so of somebody within the artworld. Although we might think of value, quite generally, as consisting of a subjective element, we principally think of it as being grounded in something else. Danto's approach allows that value is grounded in something we can perceive in an artefact – the presence of history and theory – which is the locus of its being valuable as culture *and* as commodity. However, it does require a degree of training and practice in order to perceive it – whilst it is possible that Emin's *My Bed* is not very good and its *Daily Mail* reading critics are onto something, it is more likely that those critics lack the requisite knowledge, experience and training to understand what they are looking at and thus to perceive its inherent cultural value.

Although this is far from an objective science, discourse and argument can demonstrate that Cyrus is more artistic than Snoop, for example, because she bears a meaningful relation to Kelley and Koons while he is making mere markings on a canvas completely abstracted from any history and theory of art. In this sense, value always, to some extent, resides within the artwork and is not only something that is projected onto it. Generally speaking, as should be clear by now, cultural value is usually the former, while economic value is commonly the latter. In the case of both Snoop and Cyrus, however, the mistake was that they hoped value – both economic and cultural – would be created by something extrinsic to their artworks, namely their celebrity. But, and this is crucial, Cyrus self-consciousness of what she is doing – 'gluing a bunch of junk to stuff' – gives her the upper hand because she is aware that she is making sculpture within the art-historical tradition of assemblage, thus creating a sliver of inherent cultural value.

Franco, however, is a different story. He is making things which directly respond to Hitchcock, Sherman, the history of portraiture, and thus is making art which is valuable in and of itself as art. This is why we can say with confidence that it is not very good. His celebrity affects only the price, and therefore the economic value, whereas the cultural value comes, literally speaking, from the contribution that the work makes to culture by being an episode in the story of art, which is related, in meaningful ways, to other episodes. As such, Franco's work has cultural value because it contributes to the narrative of art history; indeed, his art is born of the very fabric of art history, both using its resources and adding another layer of nuance to it. This is the cultural value that Snoop and Cyrus lack – a self-awareness that consciously places the art within an art historical context as a contribution to culture, the value of which has nothing to do with either the price it sells for or whether it is any good as art. Snoop and Cyrus are making 'art' in a bubble of their own self-indulgence with no consciousness of art historical or theoretical lineage, which blocks their work from accruing any cultural value at all. As you read this, Snoop's and Cyrus' forays into the artworld are in the distant past – perhaps now the very distant past – and consequently nobody really remembers those ventures. Indeed, you might have to Google their artworks and when you see them they will probably stir not the faintest hint of recognition because their null cultural value has ensured they are forgotten – by art, at least – as so much celebrity bluster.

It is important to remember that cultural value is a measure of the contribution an artefact makes to culture, a judgement of how much value it adds to the richness of human cultural production. Viewed in this way, it is clear that Snoop and Cyrus are making no such contribution precisely because they are haphazardly fusing materials together and hoping their celebrity will do the hard work for them. Cultural value, in the end, has to be earned; it cannot simply be created at will, which, of course, ultimately distinguishes it from economic value.

VII. Anything and Nothing At All

Why aesthetics matters more than money

If cultural value inheres in an artwork in virtue of its relation to the history and theory of art, since it is through that route that it contributes to human culture, then it seems we have arrived at the core of that which constitutes the value of art. The ground of that value is, and has to be, aesthetics, since it is that which expresses or manifests in perception history and theory, and which is the foundation for all our judgements about the meaning and value of art. For instance, although nothing had physically changed in Lancelot Thwaytes' painting, it was deemed a to be Caravaggio, and therefore valuable, in virtue of aesthetics; it is aesthetics, the way the paintings look, that makes the various Spot Paintings different from one another and therefore more or less interesting; and the reason we should want to engage with Emin's work, and the very reason her work is immensely valuable, is the way she expresses emotion through her materials, which can only ever be an aesthetic engagement with the work.

In all these cases, the grounds of our judgements, which tend to entail judgements of value, are aesthetic. It is only in the way works of art look and feel that we consider them to have any value at all. That is the crux of cultural value, but it is also the thing that the market is buying and selling and is therefore the springboard for economic value.

If we set aside almost all talk of economic value and the market, and instead focus on the aesthetic qualities of artworks and our responses to them, we will see many examples of where cultural value is the only explanation for our engagement with art. In all of the following examples, then, the value of art will be cultural, explicated on the basis of aesthetics for different reasons and logics.

For Richter or Poorer

Sometimes, the value of an artwork, as art, as culture, has nothing whatsoever to do with the identity of the artist, the work's history or its provenance, but purely to do with how the artwork looks and feels in experience. In November 2011, art critic Jerry Saltz announced on his Facebook page that he would pay anyone $155 to make him a fake Richter, Ryman, Flavin, Fontana, Duchamp, Hirst, Guyton, or Agnes Martin. A year later, he ended up with a Richter by artist Stanley Casselman. To be clear – Saltz did not want a Richter; he wanted to get as close as possible to the aesthetic experience of a Richter for a fraction of the price.

Gerhardt Richter is a titan of contemporary art who has made millions from a steady practice consisting of photorealist and abstract painting. He set an auction record at Sotheby's New York in May 2013 of $37,000,000 for a photo-realist painting of Milan's Piazza del Duomo, *Domplatz, Mailand* (1968). At the time of Saltz's challenge, Richter was the subject of a major Tate Modern retrospective and his prices had already reached $16,600,000 at auction.

In his quest to own the aesthetic experience of an expensive work of contemporary art, Saltz calculated how much he could afford for something that aesthetically resembled a Richter as closely as someone who is not Gerhard Richter could manage to produce. Saltz named a price that is completely rational: it is not so much that it only appeals to those with more money than sense; but nor is it so little that most people would not have to give it some thought before handing the money over. $155 is an amount that many people could afford to spend on something they really want, but not on a mere whim. It illustrates that the price of art is a function of what someone will pay for it, but instead of locating this in the billionaire who will pay a crazy price because they can afford it, it locates it in the person who desperately desires something and will pay at the top end of their rational capabilities for something they truly believe is worth having for reasons which have nothing to do with money.

In 2014, Richter boldly inaugurated Marian Goodman's London gallery with over 40 abstract paintings, the experience of which brought home why Saltz had set himself this challenge. The uniform enamel of the Doppelgrau paintings, pictures of nothing but grey, their glass surfaces reflecting back the entire world, are lessons in the seduction of fifty shades of grey. The swirling, bleeding colours of the Flow paintings conjure the chaos of light when you close your eyes while staring into the sun, and yet the glass surface causes the entire abstraction to recede into an otherworldly dimension of order that stands simultaneously removed from and just within the grasp of coherence. The one oil on canvas work in the show, *Abstraktes Bild 875-3* (2001), typified the kind of aesthetic immersion that art should always aim for: enchanting, enraptured loss of self in the aesthetic moment.

Richter is decent enough at what he does that one wonders why anyone, especially someone with the eye of Saltz, would want anything but the real thing. And here we get to the crux of the issue: 'the real thing' holds immense sway, for both collectors and casual viewers, but only because we care about authenticity. Authenticity has two senses here: first, the work is what it appears or purports to be; and second, that it is the product of some particular hand. Saltz is careful to maintain the first sense, prescribing that he does not want an outright forgery, but rather something that has the appearance of Richter made by someone else. But, appealing to the second sense, no matter how perfect a simulation of a Richter it may be, it is missing the crucial authority of Richter's own hand. The price of contemporary art is a figure put upon the authentic product of an artist, even if this has been diluted into the authentic product of an artist's studio. In the age of celebrity and the mass art market, authenticity – as the locus of price and the arbiter of value – has been reduced to the brand name an artist has constructed for themselves. Saltz's painting is therefore authentic in the sense that it is precisely what it purports to be, but it is inauthentic in the sense that it lacks the right branding.

It is no surprise that the astronomical price of contemporary art reflects an irrational faith in the brand, but Saltz's wilful imitation of a Richter reveals something infinitely more interesting. In focusing on the brand as an indicator of economic value, the price of art has become utterly divorced from cultural value, which is a judgement of the value of the work as an aesthetic object that a human being engages with and gains a certain worthwhile experience from. In the case of

Richter, the aesthetic effect is decent enough to warrant his being accorded cultural value as one of the noteworthy abstract painters of recent history, which is easily evidenced by works such as the *Cage 1-6* (2006) paintings. But, as far as economic value is concerned, it is the brand of Richter, and not the aesthetic experience, that you are paying for.

Richter is good, but he is not so good that $16,000,000 is a reasonable price for one of his paintings. The brand creates the illusion of cultural value and therefore justifies the prices, but when you look deeply through the surface of the canvas, you see there is nothing there that you either could not have lived without or that could not have been equally produced by somebody else. Saltz, unlike wealthy collectors, was able to disavow himself of the immensely seductive Richter brand precisely because he was interested in aesthetic effect. After all, a perennial concern of consumer culture is that some brands denote better quality than others, but the proof of that is in the consumer experience and not in the brand's self-image, marketing budget or advertising copy. A consumer knows from experience the difference in quality between an Armani suit and a Topman suit or can differentiate the feeling of driving a Ferrari from that of driving a Ford. In very simple terms, different brands feel different and part of that difference is in quality, but a great deal of it is in acumen or reputation, and there is nothing words can do to change the consumer's mind once they have experienced it for themselves.

As such, Richter is not good because the market says so, or because his studio assures you it is so; a Richter is good because it delivers a pleasurable and edifying aesthetic experience to the viewer. Furthermore, while Richter is good, if you were in the market to buy an aesthetic experience, you could do a great deal better than Richter for the same price or less: a Frank Bowling or a Barnet Newman, or even a Kiefer, would yield more, aesthetically speaking, because they possess deeper cultural value than Richter, and yet would cost the same as, or much less than, a Richter to buy. So when Saltz set his heart on the experience of a Richter, he set it appropriately low and priced it reasonably by abstracting from the experience all the noise of the brand.

Casselman showed Saltz over fifty canvases, most of which he rejected as too pretty, too deliberate or too self-conscious, but the two that made Saltz's heart skip a beat were the ones that Casselman himself rejected as mistakes. Here Saltz saw the Richterian appropriation of accident, as if Casselman – a very gifted and accomplished painter – could only make a Richter when he was not concentrating.

Casselman signed his own name on the back of the two canvases and received his fee. Saltz walked away with an affordable artwork which replicated the aesthetic experience of an unaffordable artwork. He was able to achieve this because he rightly doubted that market prices reflect what is important about art, which is something that can be reproduced by a skilled maker, since it is a matter of mere historical contingency – rather than anything like artistic genius – that Richter has branded a certain range of aesthetic objects. The fact that there is no discernible aesthetic difference between a Casselman-Richter and Richter-Richter indicates that aesthetics trumps the brand every time.

Casselman was able to make a near-perfect Richter because art is just stuff made by people for other people to experience and to enjoy, and what difference does it make if it is experienced and enjoyed just the same as its indiscernible counterpart? The fact is that it does not make a difference. Richter is good, but he is not so good that he is the only person in the world capable of producing the things he produces.

Indeed, once we see that the aesthetic experience of a Richter is the only thing that makes it valuable, we see that cultural value can be divorced from economic value with no loss of aesthetic effect, since it is contingent upon an aesthetic experience that is itself contingent on an individual being able to produce such an experience. It does not matter if that individual is Casselman or Richter, or whether it cost $155 or $38,000,000, aesthetics was the only thing we were ever searching for in the first place.

I'd Be Safe and Warm, If I was in LA

An artist's biography directly influences their aesthetic in the sense that the art they make is a product of who they have been and who they become. This much is obvious. But what is less obvious is the way in which an artist's environment is the immediate precursor to their aesthetics. In the case of David Hockney, the shapes and colours on the canvas, and their manifold effects, are the direct consequents of his being immersed in the landscapes of California and Yorkshire. Moreover, one of the things we value in art, as discussed in the case of Emin, is its expression of and connection to human emotion. Hockney is an example of how aesthetics is born from environment and meaning is born from life experience, which infuses art with a value that has nothing to do with economics.

Hockney's journey from Yorkshire to California and back again traces the aesthetic journey of his painting. He decamped to LA in 1964, having graduated from London's Royal College of Art and having been instrumental in the early days of British Pop Art. It was while living in the Hollywood Hills that he made many of his seminal works, such as *A Bigger Splash* (1967) and *American Collectors* (1968). Those early pictures were replete with the distinctive vibrancy and energy that would become his trademark, the same qualities that enabled him, many years later, to paint Yorkshire the way he did California. In 2005, when Hockney first announced his return to Yorkshire – his first full time stint since the 1970s – it was hailed as the homecoming of the decade. It was there that he turned his hand to painting the landscape in every season, creating the body of work that comprised his celebrated show at the Royal Academy, London, in 2012. It was mesmerising to see what happens when, finally, you take the Yorkshire boy out of California: the brooding English countryside comes to life in a symphony of colour that both burrows to the core of its nature and expresses the artist's sincere affection for his homeland. But the line between Mulholland Drive and the Yorkshire Wolds was so fine that not even sitting sketching in the car through grim winter after grim winter could take the California out of the boy, even if the boy was older and wiser and – geographically – far from California.

The difference between the young and the old Hockney, the early and the late work, is vast. Human figures, once so central to pictures of modern life by an original pop artist, vanished in favour of the sensuous immediacy of nature. In LA during the 60s, life was a constant party, and so the pictures were populated with people, reflecting a sociable existence, whereas Bridlington in the 21st Century was a place of quiet reflection in the twilight years, populated by fewer but closer friends and where the landscape dominated an aging man's attentions. The major difference, however, is one that transcends both geography and subject-matter, one that can only be taught by the ravages of age. Despite the urgency of his task to capture the ever-rolling seasons and the universal march of nature, Hockney seemed to paint with a transcendent calm; he was using his brush less to capture a moment of exhilaration and more to lay down a holistic view of the life-force that drives all the things youth once took for granted. It is almost as if the urgency to capture the season before it changes again is analogous to the urgency to paint everything before death catches up. The fundamental aesthetic shift in Hockney's work is not colour, subject-matter or form, but tone – from urgency to calm, fever to transcendence.

Then one night in March 2013 that calm was shattered, probably for ever. Hockney's 23-year-old assistant, Dominic Elliott, died following a 24-hour drinking binge and returning to Hockney's studio-home high on ecstasy and cocaine. Elliott joined Hockney's studio staff as an assistant, having dropped out of studying physics at the University of York. Everyone who knew Elliott found him to be a kind, gentle soul, with Hockney himself being especially fond of him and immensely proud of his help on the Royal Academy show.

Hockney's ex-boyfriend, John Fitzherbert, was the one who took Elliott to the hospital in Scarborough, having been awoken at 4am to find him standing at the end of the bed asking to be taken to hospital. He died some time during the 45-minute drive. Earlier that night, Fitzherbert reports, Elliot had become agitated, which ended with him throwing himself off a 10-foot balcony, whereupon he merely dusted himself off and agreed to go indoors with Fitzherbert.

An inquest later heard that somewhere between Fitzherbert's falling asleep and his being woken again to drive to the hospital, Elliott had drunk a lethal dose of drain cleaner containing a 95% solution of sulphuric acid. Meanwhile, Hockney was soundly sleeping in his room at the end of the hall, having retired at 9pm after a day spent painting, and would only discover what happened when his trusty assistant, JP, told him the next morning. The whole ghastly business left Hockney devastated and completely broken. The death of a young man whom he had both employed and treated as a member of his own family brought an unshakable cloud over Hockney and, ultimately, over his tenure in Bridlington.

Hockney was completely paralysed from painting for a year or more, so he moved his studio permanently back to LA to see if the Californian sun could rejuvenate his spirits as they had energised him in his youth. Hockney began painting again, producing a bold acrylic portrait of JP, which he liked so much that he went on to make 50 portraits of different people, all sitting in the studio for three days at a time. This gave rise to a new body of work, a series of ecstatic scenes of people dancing, after Matisse. Further portraits of people standing in strange formations would comprise his investigations into perspective that were shown at Annely Juda, London (2015). He also followed in the footsteps of Caravaggio and Cezanne by painting portraits of card players, while continuing to make iPad drawings of Yorkshire from memory.

The extent to which an artist's biography influences and explains their work always remains an open question to be answered on a strictly case by case basis, but in the case of Hockney, it is inescapable, especially in respect of geography and environment. The wild nature of Yorkshire led him to a zen-like study of the landscape, completely abstracted from humanity, although always living and working in warm company. In the Bridlington years, he was concerned with broad themes of nature, power, mortality and motion because that, in the passing of the seasons, was all there was to see. Bridlington grounded Hockney in the landscape, making humanity, once so prevalent in his art, a mere speck of dust on the eternal, unforgiving carousel of life that is as unstoppable as it is majestic. But the death of Dominic Elliott forced introspection on humanity itself, which resulted in a series of pictures with human subjects. Once again, LA, the quintessentially artificial landscape of capitalism, turned Hockney's attention back to humanity. It seems that the arid desert sands of California and the simulacrum of reality in LA are the optimum conditions for Hockney to interrogate the depths of the human condition, as he did with such abandon early on in his career. Where Yorkshire brought Hockney monumental nature, California brought him fragile humanity.

Philosophy, Heidegger once said, is homesickness because thinking is the attempt to learn how to dwell, how to just *be* in the world. And the same might be said of art – it is only the attempt to make peace with the world, the attempt to anchor oneself in a constantly shifting space and time.

Paintbrush Paparazzi

Stella Vine's paintings unravel the myths of contemporary celebrity, gender stereotypes and identity. But they also offer an intimate, revealing view of Vine herself, mastering the artistic technique of looking inwards while looking outwards. It is as if every picture is a self-portrait, even though the face is of someone else, and therein lies the unsettling power of her art. In Vine's work, the visual style is everything. Here we have an example of cultural value grounded in aesthetics, where the contribution to culture is an outsider's riff on the age-old art of portraiture. Vine takes the portrait to and beyond its logical limit with an aesthetic that transcends everything we think we know about painting.

Vine did not go to art school. She was a waitress, a cleaner, an actress, a single mum and a stripper, as the press never tires of reminding us. She took a few classes at Hampstead School of Art, but it never came to much; perhaps the institution of the art school, even a small, community one, did not suit her. In hindsight, it hardly seems to matter, since Vine's gifts cannot be taught and should not be ruined by education. In 2003, she decided to become her own gallerist, to learn the hard way, as she has said, 'to be Jay Jopling', so she opened a gallery, Rosy Wilde, in East London and later relocated it to an upstairs room on Soho's Wardour Street[92]. A gargantuan task for anyone, not least a Northumberland girl who paints with the abandon of a child and the penetrating insight of a psychoanalyst.

Her big break came in 2004 when she sold some works to Saatchi, whom she says she met for two or four minutes (depending upon which account you read), as if she was bound by solemn covenant to perpetuate the myth of Saatchi. One of the works bought by Saatchi was the now iconic painting, *Hi Paul, can you come over I'm really frightened* (2003), which is one of those in an artist's body of work that comes, retroactively, to be career-defining. This picture is symptomatic of her style, with its superficially naïve forms and jarring pallet, depicting Princes Diana in mid-hysteria, blood dripping from her mouth, her cheeks rosy but her hair strangely grey and sporting a crown. The furtive, impasto brush strokes, the wavy lines that are vaguely reminiscent of van Gogh and the juxtaposition of colour give it an air of carelessness, but one which is on the

---

[92] See Lynne Barber, 'Vine Times', *The Observer*, 7 July 2007.

wrong side of grotesque. It looks like a work of outsider art, and that, although Vine would surely disagree, is what it is – Vine stands outside of the artworld but within the tradition of portraiture, which is the crux of her charm.

There is something grotesque about the picture: the urgency of the painter's hand and the wilful disregard for the rules of painting convey depth of subject-matter. But without all the affectations of form, perspective, colour and light the painterly illusion of pure, unmediated aesthetic fall away, and we are left with raw human emotion, an instant of human drama which, as we know, can only end in inconsolable tragedy. Vine deconstructs portraiture to its barest elements – a subject, a gaze, an idea, a feeling – so that it feels a bit inside out, as if those internal mechanisms of a portrait are the first things to catch the eye, while everything to do with fine art and portraiture falls by the wayside.

There followed a series of lucrative solo shows, most notably an exhibition at Modern Art Oxford in 2007 which included nearly every painting she had ever made. Vine had scandalised the artworld with paintings that revel in their surface naivety; paintings, no less, of A-List and Z-List celebrities, instantly recognisable and yet curiously alienated from the tough exterior of fame, perennially vulnerable, damaged and human. In this conflation of the celebrity hierarchy itself, there is something deeply revealing, both about the fairy-tale of celebrity and about Vine herself.

Nobody could escape her brush: she painted Amy Winehouse, Courtney Love, Kate Moss, Elizabeth Taylor, Chantelle Houghton, Pussy Riot, Sienna Miller and Amy Childs. All women who are equal measure heroic and tragic in their own ways, and yet in Vine's hands the playing field is levelled so all these women wear their fame as a curse and their unbridled humanity as a virtue with no distinction between their roots or destinies. Vine challenges the constructed stereotype of the female damaged by brutal masculinity. Her women are, like herself, in the grip of an outmoded womanhood, with all its tenderness and terror in a merger of Elizabeth Wurtzel with the Spice Girls. It is Girl Power and Prozac in an effort to reclaim the woman in art not as object or muse but as subject and master.

In the midst of these starlets in the dizzying cosmos of modern celebrity, the figure of Sylvia Plath looms large as the archetypal tragic heroine who was ruined by a man. The Plath myth is as powerful as it is well-rehearsed: the femme fatale who came to England on a Fulbright Scholarship, married a thrusting young poet, wrote reams of poems about her dead father and wound up her days in an oven in Primrose Hill. But Vine does not paint Plath because she relates to the myth, but rather because she is interested in the way that women are always prefigured by their myths rather than their art. For Vine, painting such women is an attempt to burrow beneath the myths and to see beyond their professional output to uncover the struggling, cowering, terrified human being underneath the carefully constructed surfaces.

It is in this sense that one can see Vine's paintings of other people as constant, unflinching iterations of a self-portrait. She does not necessarily identify with her subjects as women or mothers or celebrities, but rather as individuals who have had their identities co-opted and battered by the world around them. This, she thinks, is a reflection of herself – Vine's own journey to fame and fortune was one in which she felt exploited as a woman, as an artist with remarkable outsider style and as a novice playing the, largely male, game of the artworld. In Vine's world, we all give so much of ourselves to others just to get by that our Selves – deep inside, behind the constant façade of the face – get lost in the seas of our public personas. And here is the great aesthetic trick of Vine's paintings: the visual style – childish, naive, folkish – enables her to get to the core of a person's being because it is pure feeling, liberated from the trappings of figuration.

This purity of expression enables her to interrogate and display the subject's soul, and every time it happens to contain granules of her own soul intermingled with that of a celebrity with whom she feels an affinity. These paintings, which initially you would be forgiven for discounting after a single glance, derive their value from the way they look in the purest sense, since it is the visual style that expresses the true meaning of the pictures.

Vine's celebrity portraits express a deep concern with the fragility of humanity, particularly as she sees it abused and perverted by celebrity, in which the artist exorcises herself through the images of the famous, who are, after all, the common property of us all. The Princess Diana paintings, for example, seem to be about an essentially good woman in turmoil, buckling under the pressure of the media spotlight, but really they are a metaphor for Vine's grief over the death of her mother. One woman's tragedy, it seems, is another's, too.

In Vine's world, celebrity is just a mechanism which enables society to pretend that some people are better or worse off than ourselves; but Vine feels herself to be in possession of the truth – that fame is a meaningless fiction because underneath we are all the same damaged, vulnerable human beings. The fact that Vine paints celebrities rather than mere civilians adds one final delicious conceit: celebrities are different from the rest of us because they have to toil their demise in public, adding one more hurt to the trials of being human.

The value industry, represented, as ever, by Saatchi, was seduced by Vine's deconstruction of portraiture, by the simplicity of the aesthetic in counterpoint to the complexity of the subject. The naïve folk-art appearance is exactly the right vehicle for an investigation of the relationships between genders, between celebrities and their admirers, between the portrait and its subject. No other aesthetic programme could have captured this timely and urgent project, and nobody other than the great Stella Vine could have pulled it off single-handed with such style, while also making a bit of money from it.

But the great paradox of it all is this: Vine's visual style is so unique and such an acquired taste that the value industry could not have seen its way to impute to it any cultural value at all if it were not for the standing possibly of economic value being generated. Vine paints in a way that does not look attractive or immediately seductive, nor does it initially appear to possess depth and substance, but the thing that drew the attention of the value industry – of Saatchi – is celebrity. These curious portraits of famous people, including the most famous of them all, Princess Diana, found their own market, not in virtue of their aesthetic programme, but because the subject-matter is in and of itself marketable.

Here is a grim illustration of how the value industry operates: the seasoned art viewer can see that Vine's paintings have cultural value in and of themselves, for all the aesthetic and thematic reasons outlined above, but if any of that – especially the surface aesthetic – is challenging, which in Vine's case it is, then the value industry must build cultural value up from a basic premise of economic value. In Vine's case, not astonishingly different from Warhol's, that basic premise is celebrity: the paintings are treated, not as works of art in and of themselves, but as celebrity portraits, as if they are hewn from the pages of glossy magazines which merely document the trials and tribulations of modern celebrity, just as Warhol manufactured images of the starlets of his day, reflecting the sticky fluidity of celebrity.

Vine, a painter of idiosyncratic style, is the paintbrush paparazzi – the 21st Century antagonist who, more vociferous than Warhol and less glamorous than Richard Philips, documents celebrity as if photography does not exist; who paints the cultural figureheads of the day as if it is still the times of court painters and cavaliers, imbuing the familiar faces of the day with a tragedy and vulnerability that the camera could only conceal. And yet, in spite of such high-minded analysis, Vine is grounded in the sensibilities and intuitions of casual observers – art lovers with nothing at stake but our taste – who can see through the shimmer of celebrity and the substance beyond the style to discern that the primary, if not the sole, point of Vine's work is aesthetic. The value industry could not concede such a contention in Vine's case because it requires too great an intellectual effort to untangle that aesthetic from the marketable and lucrative surface attributes of her celebrity subjects and folkish style.

Anything and Nothing At All

The value industry possesses a distinct skill for creating value out of nothing by transfiguring cheap or worthless materials, or mere ideas, into items of vast economic value. Now we are going to see an example of an artist who makes his work out of not very much, but creates great cultural value – so much so that he ended up creating the first great artwork of the 21st Century – although he generates extremely modest economic value for both himself and his gallerist. Indeed, Martin Creed has said that he makes 'about as much a train diver', which means, assuming the standard 50/50 split offered by commercial galleries, Hauser & Wirth also makes from Creed about as much as a train driver[93]. It is a decent living, but slim pickings in the grand scheme of blue-chip galleries. The example of Creed will illustrate the importance of aesthetics as the locus of meaning in art, since we tend to think of art as meaningful, somehow insightful, telling or edifying.

The Richters we considered earlier, for example, are fine aesthetic experiences but they are also completely meaningless, which is an entirely acceptable goal for art to aim for, even if it is not always the one we are looking for. The important point is this: whether or not an artwork generates a profound aesthetic experience or conveys an edifying meaning or message, it will still possess cultural value quite apart from any economic value. If it is to mean anything at all, it must seek to convey that through aesthetics.

Creed's work has as its subject an existential tussle between order and chaos, which draws the viewer to engage in an argument, to resolve a battle between an elegant simplicity and a maddening silliness. It is pure expressionism, masterfully dressed in the aesthetic of minimalism and conceptual art. Creed's 2001 Turner Prize winning *Work No. 227 The lights going on and off* was the first great artwork of the 21st Century because it is simple, elegant, provocative, slightly annoying, rather silly and expressive of all that occupies the human

---

[93] The 'about as much as a train driver' claim was made by Creed during a talk at the Quay Arts Centre, Isle of Wight, 18 September 2014.

condition. It does the work that art is supposed to do without any of the tiresome labour. A work of art should lead you to have some kind of insight that nothing else could generate and *The lights going on and off* excites that feeling with admirable economy. It is, to paraphrase the great Sebastian Horsley, the sensation of art without the boredom of its conveyance.

The movement between dark and light creates a rapidly fluctuating sense of panic and relief, loneliness and comfort, confusion and clarity that there is never quite time to absorb or understand. It starts off as a surprise, a moment of uncertainty and chance, but then settles into a consoling rhythm. It is, in the end, a metaphor for life and the universe: so fragile, so delicate, so surprising, so samey, ultimately just a series of seemingly random flickers that are generated by a preordained force that we can neither control nor access; the fragility and fortuity of our very existence is a series of unstoppable on/off movements that constantly catapult us between the positive and the negative. 'And what about it?', Creed seems to say, as that light continues to flicker in its empty room, giving away nothing and everything at the same time.

The lights going on and off appears to be a work of conceptual art, since it could be installed in any room on earth and still convey the same meaning; but it also seems to be a work of minimalism, consisting as it does of very little material for very great aesthetic effect. However, Creed's art is neither minimal nor conceptual because it ultimately has human expression at its core. In minimalism, the work of art is just what it is and nothing more, such that Donald Judd's boxes are just boxes hung on the wall; the artwork is all about the aesthetic experiences of the object. In conceptual art, the work of art is not what it is, but is in fact something more, namely an idea which the object only suggests or inspires, like Hirst's shark, which is an exploration of the fear of death rather than a mere zoological specimen. The outward appearance of Creed is certainly that of minimalism with a shock of colour and conceptual art with an injection of emotion. It looks like minimalism because there is nothing there but flickering lights, so it appears there is nothing other than the pure aesthetic experience. And it looks like conceptual art because the object from which it is made – a flickering bulb – is so pedestrian that the meaning of the work must be something independent of the object if it is to be thought of as profound.

Creed's trick is to maintain that the object is just what it is, but to insist that it could also be more or less than what it is, leaving all possibilities open and dictating nothing, so that, despite appearances, it is not minimal or conceptual at all. It really is just the lights going on and off in an empty room, and then there is a gap where it is less or more than that, and the gap must be closed by the viewer's emotional response. That response is always a struggle between opposites, aptly illustrated by *Work No. 200 Half the air in a given space* (1998), where a sea of balloons falters between a claustrophobic threat and a childish delight. This emotional battle, the viewer's task to fight it out themselves and the resultant feeling of exhaustion in front of the artwork are Creed's standard schtick. Even the most minimal works, like the lights, force you to navigate your way through your fury at the idea that this is a work of art and your sense that it is an act of unbridled genius. The end product, in Creed, is always the same – stuck between two opposing views, the viewer comes to their own conclusion with a sense of catharsis.

Creed is a great expressionist because he uses such simple means to evoke and provoke strong emotional responses. He presents us with an idea, a thesis, and its opposite, an antithesis, which are both embedded in the work but entirely plain to see – since there is nothing more than the object itself– and then he invites us to make something out of these ambiguous opposites. The resultant synthesis, which cannot not be reached, is our emotional response, and our emotional response – and ultimately nothing else – is the meaning of the artwork. This is both a different end and process from anything that normally happens in conceptual or minimal art, and it is for this reason that Creed's work should rightly be regarded as expressionism.

The joke about playing all the right notes but not necessarily in the right order is the perfect analogy for Creed's work: something that teeters on the cusp of failure and uncertainty ends in a meticulously executed gesture of artistic dissonance. It succeeds precisely in virtue of the fact that it eschews the high-mindedness of art as something complicated or out of the ordinary, while effortlessly achieving the prized artistic goal of engaging emotionally with the viewer, effortlessly leading to a great insight. *The lights going on and off* was the first great artwork of the 21st Century because, after a decade of excess and exuberance, it brought the artworld back down to earth by reminding us that art deals with all that is fundamentally human. At the time, it was both surprising and necessary, since art had become so awash with excess and money that it was difficult to remember what art was all about.

This is the real business of art, and as such it does not have a price, but Creed manages to make a living from it because his collectors are paying for aesthetic experiences and artefacts which are enjoyable in themselves, whether or not they care that these things have the grim striving of humanity in the face of order and chaos as their sole semantic content. This is the perfect expression of Graw's injunction that the art market must put a price on pricelessness: insofar as art is an exchangeable commodity, it must have a price attached to it, but the price is attached to the cultural value of art as an edification of the human spirit, which, if we think on it too deeply, does not make sense at all. Creed has struck gold – as least as much gold as a train driver – because he makes the kind of art we really want once we shut out the noise from the market, and thus find a market for his art, which seems, on the surface, logically unsellable.

In Creed's work, the delicate tension between cultural and economic value collapses because the artefacts are practically worthless, while the experiences they produce are priceless because they are provocative, emotional and intellectually rich, which are aesthetic experiences that culture can scarcely do without. Economic value is here constructed entirely out of cultural value, which itself is always already negated by the human gravity it carries outside of the market. Creed does this by enabling mundane, everyday objects to create aesthetic representations of our experience of life itself, which is, after all, just about an experience anything and nothing at all.

In all the cases we have here considered, aesthetics is the only thing that truly matters, since it and it alone is the source of everything else. The market may like a Richter *because* it is a Richter, but the art-loving public only like a Richter insofar as it is aesthetically pleasing, interesting or edifying. Similarly, the relationship between Hockney's biography and the interpretation of his paintings can only be accessed first from the way the paintings look, while the way Vine's paintings look is the only thing that gives them any value at all. As such, when we are talking about value – whether cultural or economic – we are talking about the value we attach to or, more circumspectly, derive from aesthetics. When viewed in this way, we can see why the art market is such an impossible proposition: aesthetics is both fundamental and priceless, so the attempt to put a price on it must be a mere construction, an affectation of capitalism which has no meaningful bearing on the practice of aesthetics. Aesthetics, in some form or another, would continue to be practiced if we did not have markets or mechanisms of exchange, which is the prospect that we finally turn our attention towards.

VIII. Gazing into the Abyss

How art can survive the market

The power of the market is waning. There was art before the boom of the 90s, and there will be art long after the market bubble bursts. It is not that prices are plummeting or that there is considerably diminished interest in buying and selling art, but in the years following the Great Crash of 2008, there was a gradual shift of emphasis. The desperation fell out of the market – buyers bought more circumspectly, and sellers held their cards closer to their inflated chests. Sometimes, the market gets it wrong: it fails to sell, promises too much, delivers too little. When this happens, art is the winner. We shall lastly consider cases where the emphasis, which always supposed to be on economic value, shifts vastly in favour of cultural value. The cultural value of art is here seen to be so obvious, so universal and so irresistible that not even the market can betray it in the end. Art can and will survive its rampant market by simply being what it is.

The Life of Brian and the Death of Art Criticism

Responsible, intellectual criticism is crucial to the survival of art. Critics are, generally speaking, as objective as it is possible to be about art in at least the sense that they should have nothing to gain from speaking insincerely about it. They are the only people from whom an honest appraisal can be sought, since gallerists, collectors, artists and curators all have something to gain from saying the right thing and everything to lose from speaking their minds.

Art needs critics because the artworld, at least that sector which has a vested interest in the financial side of things, is full of Yes-People – people who will never say no and never speak their minds – people who will say anything to close the deal, even if it is not the right thing for the integrity of art, aesthetics or culture. Terrible exhibitions happen precisely because the Yes People will not say No, such as Marc Quinn's ghastly 'The Toxic Sublime' (2015). A critic would have been able to tell Quinn it was ostentatious and tacky, lacking substance and craft, and utterly devoid of anything that could redeem it. The sculptures, oversized silver casts of shells, were the inert, ugly gestures of somebody who possesses the money to realise his dreams but lacks the creativity to dream. The YBA superstar, creator of the mesmerising Blood Head, *Self* (1991), and sculptor of the stars had fallen from grace spectacularly with that show. We need critics because they are the only people in a position to call out and condemn bad art, without which we would simply drown in lucrative bad art.

Remember when Hirst painted those pictures of parrots, oranges and flowers it was *The Guardian's* Jonathan Jones who spoke out. Agree or disagree with the judgement, it does not matter, the important thing is that critics add another voice to the otherwise monotone debate by speaking out against a commercial artworld that can be insincere, dishonest and delusional in its judgements of art. If art is to survive in the commercial artworld, where everybody says yes all the time, then it will need critics to keep speaking out, defending the integrity of art and adding an alternative point of view to the ocean of affirmation.

The death of Brian Sewell at the age of 84, after battling both a heart condition and cancer, was a great tragedy; we lost the most incisive, intellectually responsible and provocative critic of a generation[94]. It is worth pausing to consider the life of this great man and how it made him the mammoth critic he was. Sewell was born in Leicestershire in 1931 and grew up in Kensington, where he lived with his mother, Jessica, until her death (when Sewell was 65). He did not go to school until age 11, when he was enrolled in Hampstead's Haberdashers' Aske's School for Boys; prior to that, he learnt Greek and Roman mythology and gazed at the stars with his mother. Following his national service, he turned down a place at Oxford to study at the Courtauld, where he met the renowned art expert Anthony Blunt. After the Courtauld, Sewell went to work at Christie's as a prints and drawings expert, but resigned after nearly a decade when they declined to make him a director, which he claimed was because he failed to sleep with the right people. There followed a stint as an art dealer, at which he was ostentatiously unsuccessful, since he told his clients that certain artworks were too good for them.

In 1979, Blunt was revealed by Margaret Thatcher to have been a Soviet spy. On the morning of the announcement, Sewell drove Blunt to a hideaway at the home of Prof James Joll in Chiswick and refused to tell the press anything except

---

[94] On 19 September 2015.

what he had had for breakfast. With Blunt in hiding, the media spotlight fell upon Sewell, who revelled in the attention, leading Tina Brown, editor of *Tatler*, to employ him as the magazine's art critic. This led to his best-known role as art critic for the *Evening Standard*, which he began in 1984 and continued up to his death.

Sewell's two volumes of autobiography caused a rumpus by revealing his epic sexual appetite in encounters with over 1000 men[95]. That is not to say he was not discerning, since he once as a young man eschewed an advance from British diplomat turned spy, Guy Burgess, on the grounds that he was 'dirty and smelly'. He preferred the term 'queer' to 'gay' but never regarded his homosexuality as anything other than an affliction that he could not shake off. He was brought up and remained a Catholic, but had a testy relationship with the church, feeling that his homosexuality, not to mention his wild promiscuity, had driven a wedge between him and his faith.

Sewell possessed artistic talents perhaps uncommon for critics. He was an accomplished painter, having sold his work and won prizes for it. When not in church, writing or fornicating, Sewell maintained two lifelong boyish passions: dogs and cars. His endless gentle affection for his dogs was such that when he moved from Kensington to Wimbledon in 1994 he dug up the remains of eight dogs to rebury them in his new garden. Sewell loved classic cars and once claimed to have driven his signature gold Mercedes along Kensington High Street at 140mph.

---

[95] All such salacious stories in this section are drawn from Sewell's autobiographies, which were widely trawled over after his death. See Brian Sewell, *Outsider: Always Almost: Never Quite* (London: Quartet Books, 2011), and Brian Sewell, *Outsider II: Always Almost: Never Quite* (London: Quartet Books, 2012).

Sewell was often described as 'acerbic', 'withering', 'outspoken' and 'controversial' for the force and vivacity with which he expressed his opinions. He labelled Tracey Emin 'trivial', called Damien Hirst 'fucking dreadful' and wished David Hockney – the 'vulgar prankster' – would never paint again. He also said Banksy should have been put down at birth. Indeed, Sewell's litany of bugbears reads like a who's who of art: Lowry, Freud, Picasso, Warhol, Raphael were all charlatans.

While his sharp tongue gained him a certain notoriety, he was a profoundly astute critic. He liked above all else Old Master drawings and the work of Michelangelo, and could articulate the precise mechanics of how a picture works. He did not object to conceptual art as such, but only to conceptual art in which there is no technical or aesthetic grounding to the concept. He was a big fan of Jake and Dinos Chapman, proclaiming their *Fucking Hell* (2008) to be the first great artwork of the 21st century.

Sewell's intellectual rigour is anathema to the artworld. He said what he thought and meant what he said, no matter how unfashionable or offensive, regardless of ruffled feathers or strained relationships. Indeed, Sewell once said that he'd made a mess of his emotional life because 'nothing matters more than intellectual probity. The critic must be prepared to sacrifice even his closest friends'. Nobody else in the artworld would dare sacrifice relationships for the sake of intellectual probity – is it, one wonders, even desirable? Sewell thought so.

Sewell was frequently saddled with labels such as 'outspoken' and 'controversial' because he spoke out of turn with convention. He certainly had an idiosyncratic, coarse and sometimes unduly offensive way of expressing himself; denouncing, for example, Hockney as a 'vulgar prankster' is beyond the pale since it wilfully misrepresents Hockney's intentions and sentiments. But, aside from the manner of his expression, he possessed a striking grounding in, and an extraordinary breadth and depth of, art historical knowledge. He knew what he was talking about, he just had an unpalatable way of saying it. He also, unlike the willing mouthpieces of the Establishment, possessed a finely tuned intellectual and aesthetic position on art: disagreement is an absolute necessity in art, for it fosters debate and enlightenment.

Art is about exciting the passions and the only way to do this is to develop a standard against which everything else is judged and to treat that standard as objective. That is how criticism works. Everybody has a standard, wherein they behave as if it is entirely objective, for everything: all shepherd's pies are better or worse than one's mother's, pop stars are as good as or worse than Madonna, and nobody can play football better than Beckham. Quality and value may well be relative, but if we possessed no standard which provides the marker against which everything else is judged, we could hardly make pronouncements of quality and value at all. Indeed, art criticism could not take place in any other way, since something so subjective as art could not be judged at all were it not for the imposition of a standard.

Sewell's standard by which everything else was judged was essentially Michelangelo; he lived in a world where artists were either as good as or worse than Michelangelo, which worked well enough for him. In general terms, Sewell's idea was that art had to feature some successful element of technical skill or craft, such that the Chapman Brothers hand-painting hundreds of intricate little models was judged favourably and Hirst employing someone else to put a shark in a tank of formaldehyde was judged unfavourably because it lacked any craft on behalf of the artist. Somewhere in the middle are artists like Hockney, Emin and Banksy, who try to skilfully master the craft of painting – they are, in effect, trying to reach the level of Michelangelo – but fail to get even close owing to a lack of talent. Sewell was courageous in his pursuit of this standard and was an exemplary critic because of it. All critics, of course, possess a personal standard by which they judge everything, but it just so happened that Sewell's was both specific and very high. After all, no artist would choose to be judged only against Michelangelo. Sewell did not criticise to rile people, he did so because he knew if we cannot share our views and engage in debate on culture, then there is probably no hope, and he believed – like any great intellectual from Socrates to Kant to Einstein – that some things are right and some things are wrong. The intellectual life, if lived properly, has no room for insincerity or relativism. On some level, it is unrealistic to expect everybody to live the critic's life as Sewell did, but he at least taught us how to develop and maintain a critical standard, which is the cornerstone of good, responsible criticism.

In the end, Sewell considered himself an abject failure, having given up on a glittering career at Christie's and failing to write the definitive book on Michelangelo. We should give him the legacy he deserves by following his example: we should have the intellectual courage to develop and rigorously apply our own standard of correctness to remind the artworld that criticism is uniquely objective, sincere and the final arbiter of cultural value. The beauty of the subjective nature of our responses to art is that it does not matter what our standard is, only that it is applied correctly and consistently with integrity in every case. If we do this, we can inject the discourse of commercial art with the critical voice it so desperately needs to avoid a fate of sentimental mediocrity at the hands of the yes-people who will say anything to close the sale and throw integrity to the wind.

Bacon's Pound of Flesh

On the 24th anniversary of Francis Bacon's death, 28 April 2016, the artist's first definitive catalogue raisonne was published. While it includes over 100 previously unseen works and is missing a few that remain untraceable, it reveals that Bacon's reputation has been built on a few greatest hits. The willingness of collectors to sell Bacons has skewed the public idea of what Bacon is all about; the frantic buying and selling of portraits and popes has led to the broad opinion that that is all Bacon did, or at least to the view that that is what he did best. Nothing could be further from the truth. In the case of Bacon, economic value has been privileged so highly that cultural value has melted out of the picture. History, that is, has done to Bacon what fame did to Hirst.

Francis Bacon is a great artist. One of the very best of Britain, of painting, of the 20th Century. Probably, without hyperbole, one of the best artists to have ever lived. Nobody doubts that the £42,000,000 *Portrait of George Dyer Talking* with which we started, for example, is one of the masterpieces of the 20th Century[96]. It is, then, a mystery why – if these kinds of portraits are the most highly coveted works in the Bacon canon – collectors are always so eager to offload them at auction. In virtue of regular exposure to these works and the impressive prices they realise at auction, we have been

---

[96] See Chapter II, Bringing Home the Bacon.

conditioned to think these are Bacon's best works and to think that he did little else besides. It is worth considering that the market may have misled us.

The striking thing is how few paintings Bacon's reputation is built upon. It is well known that Bacon gleefully destroyed his works, going so far as to buy one of his own paintings for £55,000 from a Mayfair gallery and immediately stamping it to smithereens on the pavement outside. He would also leave rejected canvases in the cupboards of the house he rented in Tangier, going back year after year to destroy them[97]. However, the seemingly endless flurry of Bacons on the market suggests they are abundant, but in fact our collective knowledge of Bacon is based on just 180 paintings. That is a fraction of the total 584 works collected in the catalogue raisonne, so one begins to wonder about the remaining 404 paintings and why they have not made the impact of the others.

In a career spanning 60 years, 584 paintings is not bad going, considering that hundreds were destroyed and that, when not painting, Bacon devoted considerable time and energy to booze, boys and blackjack. The popular myth tells us that Bacon only painted in the mornings, leaving afternoons and evenings free for leisure, so he achieved a relatively great amount in a relatively little amount of time. Indeed, in a period of around 45 years, Velazquez produced an estimated 120 paintings, while Vermeer, in a lifetime of 43 years (and a career of around 25 years) famously only produced 35 paintings. Picasso, on the other hand, produced in excess of 50,000 artworks, of which only 1885 are paintings, in a career spanning 82 years. Of course, times for Bacon were different

---

[97] For these and other stories about destroying paintings, see Daniel Farson, *The Gilded Gutter Life of Francis Bacon* (London: Vintage, 1994).

from how they were for Velazquez or Vermeer, and Bacon's work is of an entirely different kind from Picasso's, so perhaps 584 is a respectable number of paintings for a man who was so often preoccupied with anything but painting. If only, one wonders, he spent less time roaming the streets of Soho or destroying his own work, he might have produced more, like the solitary and reserved Rothko, who managed 798 paintings in 46 years.

The greatest hits of Bacon – iconic, masterful and beguiling as they are – conceal 404 other works, including his underrated portraits of van Gogh, who is depicted on country roads and in brown fields as a weary, haggard scream of a figure. Although fairly well known, certainly by scholars, these works are, in public consciousness, secondary to the popes and portraits we know so well. Also fascinating is a particular seascape shown at Ordovas, London, in 2015 which contains a familiar Bacon figure in the middle of an unfamiliar ocean landscape painted in luscious Prussian blue. Somewhere within the catalogue raisonne there must surely be more works like these that simultaneously proffer the familiar magic of Bacon while challenging the orthodox view with a nuance of style, a change of subject or an inflection of atmosphere with which we are unfamiliar.

It is not an accident that we only know a fifth of the extant Bacons. It is a trick of history that an artist becomes known for a small proportion of their work, for the present can only convert a lifetime into an ellipsis which must constantly contain the same small sample. If you think of all the Pollocks you have ever seen, you can probably multiply that number by ten or even twenty to get at a fraction of the number of drip paintings he actually made, and that is because we simply could not handle the enormity of his output. An artist's work has to be distilled into relatively few pieces so that we can possess a clear, distinct view of the essence that exemplifies an artist. Furthermore, not everything an artist produces is important, significant or good, and much of it is a study, a rehearsal, for the main event. After all, we are aghast in the present at Hirst's manufacturing project, so we deny that all artists realistically manufacture on a mass scale because we have the historical illusion of their popular canon. Indeed, Hirst has produced considerably less than half the amount of Picasso and production has been slowing at such a rate that it seems doubtful he will ever make as much as Picasso did[98].

Bacon produced probably just the right amount, so it is a travesty that we are acquainted with so little of it. This is due in no small part to the market that circulates a few choice Bacons before our eyes like juggling balls, always repeating the same representative sample which is echoed in the museums and textbooks. The market is a machine of confirmation bias, since it never throws up an unusual or non-standard Bacon. All we have ever had is a pound of Bacon's flesh, which has been sumptuous, but he was a fulsome, complex man.

There is no doubt about the cultural value of Bacon, nor about his economic value, but the market's representation of this great artist is at best incomplete, since a complete view cannot be in the market's interests so long as economic value is assured. Here, then, there is a word of caution: for all the emphasis we have placed on collectors being custodians of art and auction houses being important mechanisms in the verification of provenance, the market – due to its primary role as a financial enterprise – cannot be trusted to represent cultural value at all, even if it generally operates more or less

---

[98] This was true at the time of writing, August 2018, but can, for obvious reasons, not be a timeless fact.

effectively as if it is doing just that. In the end, cultural value is in the eye of the beholder, as it were, and not in the eye of the market storm.

Top of the Flops

In July 2015, some very strange things happened throughout the summer sale season known as 'auction week'. It was a sure sign that times were changing: although the much-lauded art bubble was in no danger of bursting, the greed and lust of the market was certainly plateauing.

Things got off to a rocky start at Christie's when 30 lots sold at or below their low estimate and 13% of lots failed to sell at all. That sounds bad, but Christie's still netted £95,600,000 in a single night. Nonetheless, a jittery saleroom and lacklustre bidding, stilted by a distinct lack of passion, speaks volumes about the state of the market.

Among the works that failed to achieve their low estimate was Sigmar Polke's *Moonlit Landscape with Reeds* (1969), which realised £3,900,000 and Christopher Wool's *Mad Cow* (1997) at £600,000, considerably below the low estimate of £4,000,000. There is an argument that these are not major works and that Christie's had overpriced them, but it could also have been something altogether more sinister – more endemic – in the nature of the market. Every post-war and contemporary art auction features these same artists over and over again. Perhaps the market reached the point of saturation.

Given that, in the secondary market, it is the same artists every time, just different works, it is easy to become complacent about the cycle of selling. Sometimes, however, the works are important pieces, which collectors will fight for, and sometimes they are mediocre collection pieces, such as that unsold Polke. The danger is that if the hunger for these artists subsides too much and pieces sell under estimate or not at all, then overall prices could crash. Prices, after all, depend upon other prices, as well as some ineffable notion of market confidence, which seemed to be waning at that time.

The unsold lots also included four Richters, which is a curious turn of events, given that Richter is consistently one of the world's best-selling, most expensive and richest living artists. Richter is an auction house's bread and butter, so the failure of these four lots sent shivers down the secondary market's spine. Christie's Brett Gorvy wishfully attributed this unnatural turn of events to the fact that the works were 'too intellectual'. We will return to this palpably absurd claim presently.

The YBAs had a rocky night, with two Sarah Lucas works, estimated from £100,000 to £400,000, failing to sell at all. Lucas' Venice Biennale show that year had received a tepid, if not sometimes cold, reception from critics, which may explain the failure of her work to budge. Jake and Dinos Chapman enjoyed a bittersweet triumph when their seminal *Great Deeds against the Dead* (1994), once owned by Saatchi and showed in 'Sensation', sold below low estimate for £422,500 to none other than their then dealer Jay Jopling. However, a dealer protecting prices – and therefore their business interests – is very different from a collector, an enthusiast shelling out close to half a million pounds because they genuinely desire a work of art. And here is a concerning turn of events: if an artist's dealer is the only person in the room who is willing to win the bidding – or, worse, if nobody at all is – then this has a detrimental effect on cultural value, since it suggests that the work is undesirable in and of itself if the very people who have the means – the collectors in the saleroom – do not have the desire.

Over at Sotheby's that same week it was a yoyo of triumph and cataclysm. Andy Warhol's first and only hand-painted dollar bill, made in 1962, sold well above its high estimate for £20,900,000. And then something truly mystifying happened. Bacon's *Study for a Pope 1* (1961) did not sell. It was bought for $10,000,000 in 1995 and is widely thought to be one of Bacon's crucial works from the pope series, but on this occasion, it fell flat like the dead weight of art itself under all that money, resolutely failing to attract even a single bid. Not one bid. No sale.

The market explained this turn of events in the only way it understands: reporting for *The New York Times*, Scott Reyburn said, 'For those involved in the art world, the series of sales…raised questions about the bankability of some of the market's most heavily traded names'[99]. That is, the explanation for this shocking downturn in the market's otherwise dependable, predictable fortunes is due to a lack of confidence in, or perhaps even a crisis of faith in the value of certain artists, whom are normally considered sure bets as commodities of exchange rather than of aesthetic pleasure. Something, somewhere, was very wrong indeed.

In a single week of auctions in London, international trends of the art market ground to a halt. Richters and Bacons went unsold and a litany of other works crawled across the block for considerably less than they should have or were expected to. It was a big deal. It was a big deal because artists who were auction favourites were suddenly out of favour, and, if it continued that way, the entire mechanism of the

---

[99] Scott Reyburn, 'At Art Auctions, Missed Expectations for Some Big Names', *The New York Times,* 3 July 2015.

international art market would fall apart, for the whole edifice is built on the guarantees provided by Richters and Bacons. The consequences for economic value are clear, but those for cultural value less so: the worry is that the fact that certain culturally significant artists have fallen out of favour with collectors indicates that those artists are not so culturally significant after all. Fortunately, the opposite is the case.

But before we consider what follows from this turn of events, we should pause to reject the two explanations for it that have thus far been offered. Recall that Brett Gorvy said the unsold works were 'too intellectual' and Scott Reyburn claimed that collectors were starting to doubt the 'bankability' of certain artists. To respond to Gorvy first, we might observe that the commercial artworld is a universe in which there are Richters floating around as freely as oxygen: something that is mass-produced on a grand scale and appears in auction houses with clockwork frequency is unlikely to be overly intellectual, since products of intellectual labour are hard won through toil and not dashed off as quickly as the hammer hits the block. In any case, the abstract works, as we know, are more about aesthetic experience than they are about intellectual posturing, so Gorvy's claim falls flat on all counts[100]. The only real explanation is that the works are too abundant and, for once, collectors decided to pass on a Richter knowing there would be plenty of other opportunities.

As for Reyburn's claim, we should first consider the worldview it indicates: the term 'bankability' clearly betrays the idea that collectors go to auctions to buy art as an investment opportunity or as an alternative form of currency. Indeed, earlier in the same article Reyburn describes how Sotheby's

---

[100] See Chapter VII, For Richter or Poorer, for an account of the aesthetics of Richter's abstract paintings.

London presented eight Warhol dollar sign works displayed in a witty mock bank vault, explaining how it was a literal expression of the notion that 'collecting valuable art has, for some, turned into an alternative form of banking'. It should be clear by now that Reyburn is generally wrong in this, since, as a matter of empirical fact, relatively few collectors treat art in this way. As we have seen, collectors are the custodians of art history, gaining personal pleasure from a work while preserving it for posterity. And this, in fact, has nothing to do with the collector's own opinion of their pursuits – after all, death catches up with everyone, even millionaires, so a collector can do no more than be the custodian of a work of art that will surely outlive them by some generations. Some, it will turn out, collect work as an alternative form of banking, but most, as a matter of fact, do not. Indeed, it seems as if Reyburn, who is more of a market pundit than an art historian, is looking only at the numbers, so what could he be expected to know about the human individuals in the saleroom?

Even if you are inclined to reject this claim about the reasons why collectors collect, there is an internal contradiction in Reyburn's claim: if buyers are interested in bankability, then they have no logical, sound reason not to buy a Bacon, which is guaranteed bankability every single time. That is, if they doubted, even for a minute, the bankability of Bacon, then they are fools and very poor judges. So, either bankability is not the issue at all because that is not what collectors are truly interested in, or bankability is the issue but is not a legitimate reason for not buying a Bacon, in which case we still need an explanation of why it did not sell.

The concept of value with which we have been working provides a much more plausible explanation for the no-sale of Richters and Bacons. If buyers were making decisions based upon economic value, the works in question would have sold, since they have a guaranteed resale or investment value. However, buyers were, on that occasion, making purchasing decisions on the basis of a species of cultural value: whilst they were not judging the cultural value of Richter or Bacon, as such, they were judging the value of these particular pieces to their collections. As such, buyers were making aesthetic decisions on how the works on offer would fit into the rubric of their collections. This is a judgement of cultural value in the sense that it judges the work as an aesthetic whole which fits, or not, into an overall picture where its significance to culture is evidenced in relation to other works. It was not, on this occasion at least, just about having money to burn and the insatiable desire to own a stake in the artist's brand; it was about owning a work of a certain ineffable quality that compliments a collection, that stimulates the aesthetic sensibilities in a way that no other work by that artist could.

It is worth remembering that, even in a saleroom of millionaires, art will not always sell just because somebody can afford it, and even the mechanisms of the market are capable of making aesthetic decisions that hold cultural value as the key. Who knows how things will pan out in the future of the market, but if there is a developing trend of more aesthetic decisions, where collectors are concerned with cultural value, then maybe the hubris of the boom years is finally dying down. Perhaps collectors are coming to mass consciousness of the fact that they are in communion with an aesthetic phenomenon that has to chime, not with the endless clatter of the market, but with the taste and judgement of the beholder.

Gazing Balls

The philosopher Stanley Cavell once remarked that modern art is characterised by the fact that you never know whether it is sincere[101]. He was thinking about art in terms of language, whether the artist really means what they appear to be saying. Nowhere does this apply more vividly than in the work of Jeff Koons, for whom kitsch and fine art are interchangeable, always wavering between banality and acuity. In his Gazing Ball Paintings, Koons demonstrates that the most horrifying thing about his art is in fact its sincerity, and thus provides a metaphor for the whole of contemporary art[102].

It is difficult to judge Koons' art without considering the astronomical prices, the vapid explanations, Koons' inhumanly good nature, the photo-ops and reams of critical prose on how surprisingly essential his work is. All of this billows a great smokescreen over the artefacts themselves. Furthermore, like all incandescent art superstars, Koons' work has to be seen and given time to reveal itself on its own terms to be believed.

Koons vehemently insists on the inherent simplicity of his work, in that unfailingly polite, congenial way that a banker might assure you that your investments are safe. His work is all about the unforgiving postmodern melding of high and low culture, a mesh of minimalism and Pop Art that explores the liminal space between aesthetics and economics. It is art that reflects on consumerism with an entirely self-conscious flourish. The result is a body of work that is so simple that

---

[101] Stanley Cavell, 'Music Discomposed', in *Must We Say What We Mean?* 2nd edition (Cambridge: Cambridge University Press, 2002).

[102] The Gazing Ball Paintings were shown at Gagosian, New York, 9 November – 23 December 2015 and Almine Rech Gallery, London, 4 October 2016 – 21 January 2017, and then a new series at Gagosian Madison Avenue, 30 May – 24 August 2018.

Koons can sincerely assert the glib emptiness of minimalism, while opening the floodgates to a rush of criticism that either insists on the hidden – near noumenal – complexity of the work or denounces it as a shallow realisation of how too much money corrodes culture.

The reality of it is that all of this is true at the same time. Koons' art is pregnant with an unbearable emptiness, which might just be the human condition under late capitalism, and yet it also overflows with the zealous complexity of consumer culture. Mirroring the manufacturing industry that he is commenting upon, Koons has produced a great deal of work throughout his career. He has made so much work that you have to sift through the mud to find the gems, and just when your utter disgust is about to overwhelm you, the obscenity of it all is unexpectedly distilled into a near-spiritual sense that something important is being communicated.

All of these insights about Koons' work come to the fore with unexpected force in his Gazing Ball Paintings. The gazing ball – a sphere of coloured glass – was popularised by King Ludwig II of Bavaria, who set the trend for its use as an attractive garden ornament. Koons has used it to adorn classical-style sculptures, placing the shimmering blue gazing ball in the hands, for instance, of a pristine white figure of Venus. These works are cleaner, more understated than practically anything Koons has done; they resonate with quiet reflection while their delicate curves and restricted pallet feel demure. They are the best looking, most mature thing Koons has done since the hoovers and the basket balls; they are also as seductive, slick and unnervingly postmodern.

The Gazing Ball Paintings are a different, entirely more eccentric, matter. If the sculptures are essentialist and pure, the paintings are outlandish and nearly heretical. In the paintings, the same blue gazing ball is positioned on an aluminium shelf, which is improbably attached to the front of painting. When Schnabel covers the canvas in broken crockery it creates a surface for the painting and when Kiefer attaches a fighter jet to the canvas it is a sculptural addition to the meaning of the painting, but when Koons puts a gazing ball on the front of the painting it becomes a baffling, enchanting, garish imposition. And yet the madness does not stop there. The paintings in question are overblown copies of the great works of art history, including Turner, Titian, El Greco, Leonardo and Manet. The gazing ball, the same royal blue as always, seems to hover just in front of the canvas, always in central position. The effect is one of monumental incongruence – jarring, awkward, destabilising, just like the Koons we know and love. It is indecent in at least the sense that it often fails to work either aesthetically or conceptually, but it is always irresistible, beguiling in a way that eludes articulation.

Some work better than others, such as *Gazing Ball (Turner Ancient Rome)* (2015), where the fiery, autumnal hues of the painting and the blue of the ball complement one another. It also works formally because the ball appears to be floating on the surface of the water, gliding downstream towards the bridge. Whereas the *Mona Lisa's* gazing ball looks like a carbuncle growing out the girl's side, with no apparent purpose or context in the picture. There is also something unsettling about the physics of it all, of which Koons is very proud. He says, 'I engineered this and I feel really good about it, because all these things are somewhat an engineering feat'[103]. The ball, which is attached to its shelf by a rod, seems too implausibly

---

[103] Quoted in Alex Needham, 'Jeff Koons on his Gazing Ball Paintings: "It's not about copying"', *The Guardian*, 9 November 2015. All Koons quotes are from this source.

heavy compared to the painting, adding a weight, or a burden, to the seeming effortlessness of what appears to be a masterful painting. It feels, rather too obtusely, that behind what you can see there is a clumsy support structure that could collapse at any moment.

The paintings are fairly convincing copies, although Koons has taken liberties with the scale by making them much larger than life. There were 35 in the first show and now many more, with Rembrandt, Titian, El Greco, Courbet and Rubens all getting the Koons treatment. One assumes Koons will continue to make them until demand subsides. It is obvious enough that without the gazing balls the paintings would appear to be inflated, clumsy copies that look too new and too shimmering to be convincing, but with the gazing balls they are enchanting and completely earnest, for Koons seems to be presenting them without a hint of irony. He is rethinking the canon of art history, following in the footsteps of Duchamp's *LHOOQ* (1919), but also adding something – an idea, an aesthetic, an expanded field of experience – to the canon. He says they 'are all handmade paintings…These are as exact replicas visually as the originals, they're different in size, they're flat…because they're just the idea of the painting. This is just the idea of the *Mona Lisa*'. It seems as if he intends them to be both faithful copies and conceptual gestures; a representation of the picture's essence rather than an identical copy of the picture itself. Koons is just engaging in appropriation, which is as old as art itself, but in so doing he is also rethinking art history by presenting its essential being.

The point of the gazing ball paintings, however, is something else entirely, as Koons explains with yet more irresistible soundbites: it is not about copies but about the participation of the viewer, for 'This experience is about you…your desires, your interests, your participation, your relationship with this image'. One of the interesting things about Koons is that although his work looks overblown and self-indulgent, he has an uncannily convincing way of bringing it back to the viewer's experience. Kitsch, after all, is about stirring our nostalgia for a past that we can never again inhabit; it is about putting the viewer in a position of reflection on the past and its relationship to the present, which is essentially an exercise in emotion memory. It is as if Koons is that rarity in contemporary art – an artist who makes art for the audience, with the audience's feelings and tastes in mind, which he goes to great personal trouble to explain and exemplify at every stage. Anyone who has ever heard Koons speak will recognise his tone, which falls halfway between a sage in an impassioned trance and an enigmatic life coach, expressing with the utmost sincerity his insistence on the experience of the viewer.

This sincerity is the conceptual content of Koons's work. He wants the viewer, for their own good, to have a profoundly new engagement with the everyday, with banality, which is where his pop art sensibilities reside. In the case of the Gazing Ball Paintings, he wants to viewer to have a different and enlightening experience of the everydayness of art history; he wants the viewer to rethink all over again those works with which they are so familiar. This, he thinks, is essentially a public service because he is enabling the viewer to renovate their quotidian engagement with the world, finding beauty and meaning in the gloomy everyday nothingness.

The surprising thing about Koons, then, is not the money, or the garishness, or his indulgence, but the fact that he sincerely believes in what he is doing. He does exactly what Cavell doubts art could do: Koons and his art are sincere, which amounts to the notion that he says what he means and means what he says exactly because he has a genuine desire to convene with his audience. There is nothing more to the Gazing Ball Paintings than a desire to give the viewer the idea of a great painting, on the one hand, and to create a space in which the viewer and the world are reflected back through the gazing ball itself. The experience is transcendent, simultaneously a contemplation of art and the self. This is the totality of what Koons says and means with these paintings. There is nothing ironic, cynical, obscure or intellectual, just exactly and only what it appears to be.[104].

Koons and Hirst alike are both somewhat afflicted by their sincerity, since a braying public often finds it inescapably obscured by the money, but it is safe to assume that most – if not all – art is sincere in at least the sense that its apparent message (whatever we take that to be) is conveyed and meant sincerely by the artist. Unless we are engaging in an act of philosophical scepticism, as Cavell was, we have no reason to doubt it. Artists make work because they have *something* to say and as such they sincerely mean what they say. Richter, unlike Kiefer, has nothing to say about the profound issues facing humanity, or unlike Emin who wants to tell a personal story. Richter has nothing to say about himself or the people around him, but he does have something to say about the nature of painting, abstraction and colour. And, insofar as he says it at all, he means what he says, and he says what he means.

This puts art in a curious position as regards the market. In the course of our investigations here, we have often seen cases where the market seems to have had the upper hand over art, such as when prices are used to denote a judgement of

---

[104] This echoes the earlier analysis of Hirst, which claimed that Hirst's meaning is always transparent in the aesthetics of his materials. See Chapter V, We Need to Talk about Damien.

quality or where the market makes judgements of authenticity or where the myth of money and celebrity overwrite the aesthetic impact of the art. All of this happens, but in the end art always has the upper hand.

Part of this has to do with the relationship between art and the market, which is not entirely reciprocal: the market needs art by definition because it is the art market; and art depends upon the market in the sense that the edifice of art's economy is built upon it, since livelihoods are parasitic upon it. However, art does not need the market in the sense that if the market ceased to exist, aside from the human or economic consequences, art could be disseminated and exchanged in other ways. Certainly, people would continue to make and to consume art without any kind of extant market.

The other part of the reason why art wins out over the market is that art is capable of being sincere and it more or less delivers sincerity every time. At the very least, and at the bedrock of all art, there is the sincere desire, on the part of the artist, to deliver an aesthetic experience of some kind or another. The market, however, is not capable of sincerity, or at least it is not possible to regard the market as sincere because, by its very nature, it is centrally about money. A gallerist may say an artwork is important or good or significant, but surely they will say anything to make the sale, one might think and therefore one could never truly trust either the gallerist's words or motives even if they are, in fact, sincere. Markets are made up of complex webs of relationships, all of which depend upon one another in infinitely discrete ways, so a great deal of what is said is designed to protect those relationships rather than to necessarily speak the truth.

Art is capable of sincerity, which is absolutely central to all communion, whereas the market is not. When you gaze long into the abyss of the market, it gazes back at you, but when you gaze long into the abyss of art, the abyss winks back.

The Balloon Monkey is Not What It Seems

We have grown so accustomed to astronomical prices that contemporary art, which should be surprising and fresh every time, now fails to surprise at all. In November 2014, four days of auctions in New York raised $1,660,000,000. That is around one 50th of the total value of the global art market for that whole year. The numbers are staggering, but the artworld is numb, desensitised, anaemic. One wonders how long it can go on like this and whether anybody has thought through the prospects for long-term sustainability.

Charlotte Burns points to three ways in which this economic boom seems as if it should lead to cultural bust[105]. First, the fact that commercial galleries occupy prime real estate in expensive cities such as London, New York and Paris means that artists are under pressure to make big expensive work to fund their dealers' lavish property investments. Second, the demand from collectors is so high that artists are so preoccupied with fulfilling orders for their classic pieces that they scarcely have the time or space to create meaningful new work. And third, the dynamic of supply and demand has almost entirely closed the gap between the artists people are talking about and the artists who are raking in the cash, so critics no longer head an industry of ideas in which there is a distinction between who is interesting and who is performing well on the market.

---

[105] Burns, 'Year of Record Sales, But at What Cost to the Art?'

If artists are merely making work to fund the existence of galleries, demand from collectors is obstructing the creative process and there is no longer a critical distinction between aesthetically interesting and commercially successful art, then it would seem to be the end of days for art. And this is where we began: the price of art, the ease of its circulation, the celebrity of artists, the power of gallerists and collectors have all eroded the distinction between good art and expensive art. Sometimes, it seems, art is expensive because it has to fund the continued existence of the marked and, as such, the market deems the art to be good, which seems to be more a moral claim than an aesthetic one. While an artwork occasionally deserves its price, such as a given Bacon, often the price is a function of the amount the market (broadly construed) needs to make in order to keep turning over. Sometimes cultural and economic value converge, but when they do not it is because the market is focused on things that concern markets – the exchange of goods and money – which have nothing at all to do with art.

Moreover, Burns' three factors affecting art in the market – which are very real features of the contemporary artworld – fly in the face of our pretheoretical view that art exists and persists for reasons other than financial gain. Art, on this grim view, has reached its terminal crisis: co-opted by a few megalomaniac gallerists, it can no longer perform its social function to provide aesthetic respite from the madness of human striving; and artists, seduced by the promise of riches, can no longer refuse artistically unsound but financially delectable propositions in order to follow their passions.

Sometimes an artist will try to resist the market commodification of their work. Wade Guyton performed an ontological trick on his *Untitled* (2005) by reprinting multiple copies right before it was sold at auction in May 2014. Sudden, unanticipated abundance was supposed to devalue the work by illustrating the mechanical reproducibility of the artform, thus demolishing the uniqueness that Christie's was trading on. But collectors are not careful metaphysicians and auction houses are Cartesian evil demons, so Guyton's stunt did nothing to quell the desperation in the saleroom. It still sold for $3,500,000.

Resistance seems futile because the market's astonishing indifference to the cultural value of art leads it to treat artworks as indistinct commodities; the Guyton, for example, is denied its ontological status as a mechanically reproducible work, which is what makes a particular instantiation valuable, thus side-lining the central aesthetic interest of the artist's practice in favour of economic concerns. This represents an existential threat to art, but it is no good looking to the market to neutralise it; rather, it is up to artists to do something to shake market confidence, as Guyton did. Critics can also play a meaningful role here by exposing instances in which price and quality silently divorce under the racket of the auctioneer's hammer. We must believe we have this power and we must exert it at all costs.

The balloon monkey with which we began – Koons' 19.5-foot tall orange stainless steel monolith that once presided over business in the foyer of Christie's New York – is an impeccable illustration of this state of affairs. It was commissioned by collector Frank Cohen, who could not resist the tantalising prospect of its gleaming surfaces and epic proportions. But when Koons finished making the work, after seven years of toil of almost biblical proportions, by which time Cohen had opened a swish gallery in Bloomsbury, London, to house his collection, Cohen discovered he did not, after all, have room to house the exotic beast. Although

Cohen's pockets were deep, his eyes were bigger than his gallery's stomach, so the work had to be sold on immediately as so much surplus value. *Balloon Monkey (Orange)* was swiftly transferred from Koons' studio to Christie's HQ, where it eventually sold for $25,950,000.

It looks as if the market, like collectors' desires and blue-chip artworks, will continue to inflate and there is nothing that can deflate it. The market was undented by the collector's disappointment, which only precipitated the work changing hands and money recirculating accordingly. But there is something else going on here. Although the balloon monkey seems to confirm the market's dominance, all is not as it seems, for it actually heralds a gentle shift in emphasis that nobody expected from such a monolith of an artwork.

The balloon monkey shows how art – against all odds and expectations – finally grew too big for the market. It would be naive to think of Frank Cohen as an art-lover with big dreams who was forced to turn to the market in his hour of need and who was thus used by the market as a pawn in a spectacular assertion of dominance. Cohen, as a millionaire collector, is himself a willing arm of the market with the ability to commission the world's most expensive living artist to make an epic artwork. As it turned out – against all odds and expectations – Cohen was the victim of art's hard-won victory over the market because he had ambitions that were considerably outstripped by his capabilities. Although he had the money to pay Koons, he lacked the space for the work, rendering it utterly useless to him. Suddenly art was more than the market could handle.

The market, it seemed, could dream big and art could deliver those dreams; but in the end, the market simply could not deal with the enormity of its dreams. Art knows no limitations, it possesses no mechanism by which its possibilities are outstripped by human imagination, whereas the market – despite the impression it creates with its narrative of dominance – is limited by the one thing that essentially defines it; the market, no matter what its participants can conceive of or dream up, is finite, bounded by the finite sums of money that anyone may possess, whereby those sums of money – no matter how huge or unimaginable – can only buy so much art, gallery space or storage until it is outstripped by the infinite creativity of art. In the final analysis, art has the upper hand over the market because human creativity and the ways of instantiating it are infinite in possibility. Art can produce whatever the collector can imagine, but the market cannot necessarily accommodate those imaginings.

Art will survive the market precisely because it is necessary whereas the market is only ever contingent. So long as there are human civilisations, there will always be some form of art because it is inbuilt in the human psyche to create and to express in forms that are removed from utility, that aim for the elicitation of intellectual and aesthetic insight, and, ultimately, pleasure. The market, however, is just a means of exchanging art from one person to another, a means of generating an economy from art, which could be done in other ways, even if those ways are currently inconceivable to late capitalism. As such, the value of art will always be primarily cultural, even if for a long period of its history it appears to be economic.

The dominance of economic over cultural value is an illusion, albeit an illusion that is necessary to capitalism. It is an illusion because humanity needs art, or at least some form of culture, in order to flourish, but culture does not need to be exchanged in anything like the manner of the market. The reason for this is simple: culture is that which people without millions – that is, the majority – value about art, whereas economics – whilst real and pervasive – is the preserve of the very few. Even we add up all the struggling artists who benefit from the market in some way and add them to all the millionaires in the mix, we still have far fewer people in that category than we do in the category of people who just simply consume and enjoy culture without any meaningful economic connection to it.

It has often been said that the Great Crash of 2008 did not change the fabric of capitalist societies one iota. It only rocked the boat as we sailed through a stormy patch, ultimately leaving the rest of the ocean untouched. The art market and the persistence of economic value demonstrate the unwavering grip of money and economic systems on culture, but it fortuitously transpired that culture is remarkably resilient because it is the necessity in a sea of contingency. The balloon monkey testifies to that resilience, but it is also a reminder that, when the celebrations are over and all the exotic creatures, captured and incarcerated by the empire of the market, have escaped the menagerie, art transcends the market.

About the Author

Daniel Barnes is a philosopher, curator and teacher. He gained his PhD from the University of Nottingham with a thesis on aesthetic realism and the Heidegger/Schapiro debate over van Gogh's shoes. He has taught philosophy at the University of Nottingham and aesthetic theory at Chelsea College of Art, and has delivered courses on art and capitalism (London School of Philosophy), and the aesthetics of digital art (Kristin Hjellegjerde Gallery). He was contemporary art critic for *Aesthetica* and *this is tomorrow*, and wrote columns on the art market for *FAD* and *State/f22*. At a high point in his career, Barnes was resident philosopher for *The Butcher's Apron* radio show and wrote an unphilosophical lifestyle column for *Winq*. As a curator, Barnes has worked on a range of group and solo exhibitions, including celebrated shows with Richard Stone and Benedict Redgrove.

danielbarnes.org